EARTHSPIRIT!

By

Christian R. Komor

Charlie Wehrley

Thomas F. Crum

John R. Otterbacher

EARTHSPIRIT! © 2012 by Dr. Christian R. Komor. All material in this book is, unless otherwise stated, the property of the author. Copyright and other intellectual property laws protect these materials. You may not, except with express written permission, distribute or commercially exploit the content. Nor may you transmit it or store it in any form written or electronic. Reproduction or retransmission of the materials, in whole or in part, in any manner, without the prior written consent of the copyright holder, is a violation of copyright law. Users may not distribute such copies to others, whether or not in electronic form, whether or not for a charge or other consideration, without prior written consent of the copyright holder of the materials. Some of the material contained in this publication may be found elsewhere in electronic form. Any electronic representations of this work are included within this copyright and all rights are thus reserved. Any redistribution or reproduction of part or all of the contents of this work in any form is prohibited with the following exceptions:

(1) You may print or download to a local hard disk extracts which must not exceed one page in length for the purpose of creating published reviews, critiques, analyses, instructional material or reports which will be disseminated in a public forum such as a newspaper, magazine, blog, online magazine or other electronic publication. In all such cases you must include:
- The original copyright notice as it appears here and,
- Reference to the original source of the material and where it can be obtained.

(2) You may share website links related to this material by using any of the share icons at the bottom of each page (Google Mail, Blogger, Twitter, Facebook, GoogleBuzz); Providing a back-link or the URL of the content you wish to disseminate; and, or quoting extracts from the electronic material of website with attribution to www.keiglobal.com

Contact information for questions regarding this copyright notice or for requests for permission to reproduce or distribute materials available through this protected material may be directed to Christian R. Komor, Psy.D., KEI Global, P.O. Box 6654, Grand Rapids, MI 49516 or ckomor@keiglobal.com

Library of Congress Cataloging in Publication Data

Komor, Christian R., 1959-
EARTHSPIRIT!

By Christian R. Komor.
p.   cm.
includes bibliographic references.

1. Anxiety 2. Self-Help

I. Title.
RC569.5.WW67K66   2012
616.85'2 – dc20   92-13568

ISBN-13: 9780615599106

ISBN-10: 0615599109

CIP

Publisher: KEI GLOBAL, P.O. Box 6025, Grand Rapids, Michigan 49516

Dedication

My portion of this effort is dedicated to my son Thomas who gives me hope for this beautiful Earth – and for our beautiful hearts – and to the woman in my future I have not met yet but already hold a place for.

- Christian R. Komor

Individual books by the authors are available online or through your local bookseller:

"Sailing Grace" by John R. Otterbacher

"Soulshine" by Charlie Wehrley

"The Magic of Conflict" by Thomas F. Crum

"The Power of Being" by Christian R. Komor

Canvas and print reproductions of the photographs in EarthSpirit! are available at:

www.komorearthimages.com

Copyright © 2012 by Dr. Christian R. Komor all rights reserved. Federal copyright law prohibits unauthorized reproduction by any means and imposes fines up to $25,000 for violation. No part of this material or any of its contents including images or drawings may be reproduced, copied, modified, or adapted, without the prior written consent of the authors for any purpose with the exception of brief quotations in critical reviews which must include reference to this copyright notice and URL. This website itself may be shared by any of the following means: (1) Using any of the share icons at the bottom of each page (Google Mail, Blogger, Twitter, Facebook, Google Buzz), (2) Providing others with a back-link or the URL of the content you wish to disseminate, (3) You may quote extracts from the website with attribution to **www.keiglobal.com.** For any other mode of sharing, please contact the lead author at dr.komor@gmail.com

LEAD AUTHOR'S FORWARD

"Do you have the patience to wait until your mud settles and the water is clear? Can you remain unmoving until the right action arises by itself?" — Lao-Tsu

More than twenty years have passed since the forerunner of this book, "The Power of Being" was published. In the years that have intervened I am not sure how much I have learned or forgotten about the nature of Being – you, the reader will have to be the judge of that. I am sure I have learned about pain. When I penned The Power of Being I had struggled some, leaving a challenging home setting at age 17, earning an undergraduate diploma in two years, completing a difficult doctoral degree, working for years in the nation's largest maximum security prison – the usual broken bones and broken hearts of life. I did not know, however, about real pain. That came wrapped in a gift – the birth of my son in 1994 born 3 ½ months too soon.

At birth Thomas weighed a little over one pound and his doctors estimated he had only a 20% chance of survival. The months of intensive care hospitalization and diagnosis of cerebral palsy that followed triggered in me as a father a largely dormant neurological condition in the cortical-thalamic-striatal region of the brain called Obsessive Compulsive Disorder. Within a few years my errant physiology had me struggling in a nightmare of fear, control, and compulsive behavior. (A fellow OCD-sufferer and combat decorated Army Ranger once told me he would rather be fighting in a real war any day than with OCD.)

Almost as troubling as the physical disorder of OCD, I had also been exposed to a new world-view – one that included the very real, in-your-face awareness of suffering and death with a promise that, as a mortal human, I was destined to see more. How could I ever feel safe, or more importantly let go into the blissful garden of Being I had discovered and written about all those years before when life could, randomly and without warning, plunge anyone at any time into a pit of torment and terror? The universe had upped the ante in my quest to know the bliss of Being. It turns out there were land-mines in the garden

I love movies and it was a contemporary war movie, "Black Hawk Down" that brought me an answer. In one graphic battle scene, while most of the characters are running about dodging bullets and rockets, one Sargent is just calmly going about his duties. He doesn't duck his head or run for cover - he is simply surrendering to the flow of fate. "Whatever happens will happen", he seems to say in every calm gesture and confident movement, "I only own this moment and I just do what I do – everything else I do not control."

*Sure, it's only a movie, but I knew I had found the doorway to the next level of understanding. The power of Being – that sweet, heady experience of giving oneself over to the spontaneous living of the moment – cannot truly be ours unless we are willing to go **all** the way with it. To walk with a certainty that somewhere there is a (metaphorical) "bullet with our name on it" – that none of us get out of this life alive! We don't let go into the flow of life with the faith that "God will make everything turn out all right". We do so by embracing that some things will **not** turn out all right. We let go of judging events to be "good" or "bad" and instead view them as "adventures" – with a continuing sense of open acceptance, and the knowledge that "This is my one moment for now. I can only control my next choice. All my striving, forcing, scheduling and needing and wanting it to be the other way are all sound and fury - signifying nothing. I have only two* *choices in the game of life (a game which ends for everybody) – live it on my knees in contracted in the terror at a random and sometimes cruel existence – or flowing with the energies and currents of aliveness and standing with pride." Two entirely different "adventures" illustrate my point.*

One night some years back I took my son, then seven years old with brilliant intelligence, shining compassion and a sparkling loving heart (now walking independently with canes), to a favorite spot for dinner "Just us guys." Later in the evening Thomas asked to visit a nearby water fountain. Ignoring my watch and my urge to "stay on schedule" and pushing my idea of what we "should" be doing and how fast and where we should be going - I just kept relaxing and tuning into the little things of the moment and trying to see Thomas' innocence. I gradually, perhaps against my will, began to be ok with flowing with the moment. The rest of the evening was one of those magical "back in the Garden of Eden" times as Thomas and I went to the top of the building and looked at the lights of the city and listened to a piano player that made Thomas sad and put him in a dreamy bubble of rapture for the piano playing and took a free ride with a limousine driver with nothing better to do. Somewhere along the line I think I stopped controlling the moment and just let it unfold. Ahhh - **This was Being!**

Several years later I was walking with a heavy pack and helmet light at night through the desert as part of a Search & Rescue team looking for a lost two year old boy. A thunderstorm had rolled in and we were having lightning strikes all around us causing vipers, scorpions, tarantulas and the like to surface from their burrows. Death from above and death from below, on a quest for a child who was probably dead as well. As I became aware of the pain of a bite in my right ankle I felt a peaceful joy - **This too was Being!**

I have chosen the other writers in EarthSpirit! with the hope that - as they have so often for me- they will share with you their courageous ability to let go and BE in the face of all the "slings and arrows of outrageous fortune" that life can throw at us.

Dr. Christian R. Komor
May 2012

"All motion is a denial of the overwhelming sweetness of the present moment."

- John R. Otterbacher

"Nature is the Art of God" - Dante

Many native cultures believed that the creative force behind the Universe (that sacred force which many of us understand as God) was present in all places at once and in all things of nature. If so, then nature itself is our most direct connection to God and our own source of Being. Many of us, however, lose this connection in the deepening din of electronically generated sounds and images. Riding in our machines, walking on our concrete, metal and synthetic fibers, breathing processed air, eating chemically-engineered food, bolstered by laboratory-born medicines and vitamins it is possible to go an entire day without real physical contact with anything of nature.

Humankind dominates the Earth, yet seldom touches her, feels her breath, stops for a conversation with her. Most of us do not take the time to BE with her. Even the Earths more spectacular gifts, those that should rivet our attention - the most amazing sunset, a flight of bats moving overhead, a wild storm, snowcapped peaks beneath our aircraft, fail to drawn our attention – we have seen better computer-generated effects on a movie screen. "Human doings" who are always in motion, we have forgotten how to Be with the Earth. Without our Earth Connection, driven by our own anxieties, lost in a swirl of thoughts and the crush of the world around us we are adrift. We become capable of not noticing the exhaust billowing from our idling automobile, driving in ways that threaten other's lives, breaking the rules of God and man to get ahead in the race of rats. We forget that the Earth is everything – she is beautiful life if we dance with her, and she can be unforgiving if we dance against her.

*To survive much longer as a race we must restore our connection to **Being** human, **Being** in connection with nature, **Being** who we really are with others and with ourselves. Restoring this connection – this **Power of Being** – is the mission of **EarthSpirit!** The images of nature you will find here have been left in as natural a state as possible - artificially manipulated only if necessary to bring the experience of the location accurately to you through color and light. The words are as raw and heartfelt as they are eloquent. It is our hope these images can serve as a touchstone, a reminder, a reawakening point to lead us each back to our own Power of Being.*
Peace in Your Heart and Fortune in Your Steps,

- **Christian R. Komor**, *Sedona Arizona*

THE PULL OF BEAUTY

***B**eauty calls you out beyond the contracted self, invites immersion in the larger, unseen Self. On this silver night she whispers...*
>Wake up, John
>>Wake up

— *John R. Otterbacher*

COME BACK TO CENTER...

Choose to come to the center of any storm, receiving the energy it brings. Strive to approach life from a place of discovery, without judgment. Use the energy of the Earth with gratitude for the possibility of a new twist or two of creativity, letting the energy of life in. Let it surge through your body recharging your being. Breathe, eat, speak, and act with the energy and elegance from that deep bonding to the earth upon which we walk.

-Thomas F. Crum

CENTER AND RELAX COMPLETELY

"Nature always wears the colors of the spirit." – Ralph Waldo Emerson

The twin acts of "Centering" and "Relaxing Completely" go together like ice cream and a spoon. We cannot live well without some degree of mastery of these two principles. Centering is a true mind/body experience in which we place our mental and visceral focus on the center point of our physical body mass. Known for centuries as the "hara" – this center point is an inch or two below the naval and in the center of the abdomen. Just as you can hold out your hand in front of you and feel the sensation of opening and closing your fingers, you can develop a "feel" for this center point in your body.

In order to "test" one's centered state, simply ask someone to stand side-by-side with you and give you a gentle push backward on your upper chest followed by a gentle push forward on your upper back. Your immediate tendency will be to become aware of the touch on your shoulder. This is a metaphor for the way in which thoughts of the past and future can distract us from our purpose. When this distraction occurs do not resist your friend's touch - this will only get you more caught up in it. Instead, just refocus your attention on your center point! Detach...Let go...Center!

In daily life, when we focus on center our attention is brought back to our own experience, our own self. In a centered state we neither overreach and control nor retreat and react. We stand straight - self-possessed in internal and interpersonal balance. Our focus is powerfully shifted back onto the moment – all that we really possess.

and contracted. As we contract and constrict physically and emotionally we diminish our power and lose ourselves. Tension is always a reaction not a pro-action.

There is no situation, mental, physical, emotional, spiritual, social, or political that is helped by tension. Most situations are helped by relaxation. When we relax we become like water – fluid, flowing and dynamic, able to roll with the punches of life and "take the hit as a gift." There is no end to the good that relaxing can do.

When in doubt always center and relax and you will find your way back into a natural state in harmony with nature and the Earth!

- Christian R. Komor

SELF AND SPIRIT

"*The human condition is one of perceived separation from the world around us, and from the Ground of all being, Spirit itself. This sense of separateness is compounded by those who would pit body against soul, nature against man. Our job is to transcend this illusory divide between body and soul, between our humanity and the natural world, and -- ultimately -- between Self and Spirit.*"

- John R. Otterbacher

THE MEANING OF LIFE

What is your purpose in life? To love well! That's it. And you share that same purpose with every human being across this entire world. We are all created with the divine purpose to love as well-- and as creatively-- as we possibly can. To love well is an individual art; a way of uniquely being as we settle comfortably into our own skin and begin the process of sharing ourselves and our love with all those persons we encounter across our lifetimes.

Every career path, every retirement path and every other path in life calls us to love well—in our own individual ways-- for the betterment of everyone. It is therefore impossible for you to outlive your purpose. It's inherently part of who you are. We all can continue to love well until we breathe our very last breath into the lungs of the universe.

The greatest gift we can give and receive is love. Forget the other stuff. Love last forever. Supreme Love knows no limits or conditions. It has no expectations and makes no assumptions. Real love sees beyond behavior and casts out all fear, all criticism, all harsh judgments, all resentments and all hatred.

In order for people to love us, however, they have to understand us. To understand us they need to know us. We have to be vulnerable enough to open up our hearts, look inside and come to understand ourselves. We can then paint an authentic portrait of who we are and frame ourselves in such a way that our lives make sense to us and others.

Those who like the authentic portrait we paint of ourselves and those who understand the way in which we have framed our lives, will grow to love us just as we are.

These are the people we want to add to the portrait that we savor as family and friends. These are the people who matter. These are the people we want to spend our days with. Bring the beauty within you to the surface and share your authentic portrait with those you love today—and allow them to love you back. So open your heart to Love's limitless possibilities and you will indeed become the very change you most wish to see in the world around you.

- Charlie Wehrley

ECOLOGY

'The desert is beautiful in that somewhere it hides a well." – Antoine de Saint-Exupery

Sometimes we forget what "ecology" is all about. Ecology is not about conservation, nor is it about preservation. Ecology is about balance and interrelationship. Earth **and** sky. Water **and** fire. Night **and** day. Birth **and** death. Give **and** take. All things in the known universe are in balance with one another – sometimes a very delicate balance.

While an ecosystem can normally sustain imbalance for brief periods of time, in the long-run it must find balance. The same is true in relationships. Relationships are a give and take – an exchange of time, energy, passion, commitment, and love. When we give too much and receive too little the ecology of the relationship is imbalanced. When we take too much and give too little the same will happen. Like anything else, a relationship out of balance is eventually doomed.

Some of us are prone to give too much. It may be difficult for us to even conceive of how to shift roles and accept love or caring from another person. Perhaps we have been wounded and can't find the way to open up and receive and so we give what we should be receiving. Some of us take too much and need to retrain ourselves to give. We need to have that sense of balance and equality or the ecology of our relationship will falter.

All of life in balance – and we ourselves most of all!

- Christian Komor

CHANGE

Change is a constant fact of life. We are actually powerless over change for the most part; and when we do try to control it, we ensure our own misery, because it's impossible to stop life from changing. So let's look at change this way. Change ensures life is forever new, that we are always able to grow into fresh opportunities, into higher levels of understanding, intelligence, emotional maturity, spiritual enlightenment and physical fortitude. Change also ensures we are ever-evolving in the fulfillment of loving well—and allowing ourselves to be loved well.

Growing pains are part of the process, but they are only intolerable if we offer resistance. Instead of fighting changes in our lives, we need to flow with them. Be open to the belief that change is for your benefit. Look at the bigger picture of life and realize that change is essential to your ever-evolving journey from newborn to child; from child to young adult; from young adult to adult; and from adult to full maturity.

Believe change is always for your benefit; believe in your abilities to grow with life each day; and joyfully flow into the newness of each day, into the newness of you. You may need a helping hand during your growing process. That's OK. No one grows into individual fulfillment all by themselves. So reach for that hand, embrace its warmth, and understand that personal growth is shared for the benefit of all.

–Charlie Wehrley

RELATIONSHIP

Lasting relationships have strong foundations, and those foundations are built gradually from within. They're built by two people who are willing to be sincerely vulnerable—emotionally naked, completely honest and genuinely truthful-- before each other. They're built by people who recognize their individual limitations, and own them the same way they own their personal assets.

These are people who honestly say to each other "Here I am. This is the REAL me. Love me as I am and I will love you as you are. Together, let's build a strong relationship at will weather the sandstorms of our shortcomings and thrive on the rainbows of our strengths. Accept me as I am.

You will notice that none of this has to do so much with physical beauty as it does with inner-beauty that can sometimes be expressed in physical ways. Let's face it. We can be in lust with multiple people every day of the week, but we won't find ourselves being in love with any of them. Love requires more than lust. Love requires taking time to really know someone, taking time to understand them and arriving at that spiritual place where God brings two souls together and unites them forever as soul mates. Soul mates love beyond the beauty that the eye can see. Soul mates love on a fully integrated physical and spiritual plain.

- Charlie Wehrley

HEART WISDOM

Emotionally mature people long to hold hands physically, but even more so, they long to hold the hands inside each other. They long to hold hands within by sharing the truest inner-workings of their hearts. They want to share their every fear, their every discomfort, their every quirk—their total dark side with the other, knowing that they will be accepted and loved despite all of their imperfections by the other.

If you long for such genuine intimacy, such tremendous freedom to be the very person that God created you to be, then start by being genuine with yourself. Make a decision to be completely open with yourself and then with someone who feels safe. The most valuable element in any relationship is the sharing of self. The beauty is in discovering the sacred essence inside the other. We all have to be able to give that much of ourselves to each other if a relationship is to bloom, blossom and grow in spiritual beauty. Think about what you are giving to your relationships. If you are giving everything but yourself, then take a step back and discover who you are inside, become comfortable with that person inside of you, and start to share that person with the others in your life. The spiritual element of a person is what we fall in love with. It's what holds our interest and attention. It's what makes one face different from all the others, and thus essential to our lives.

That spiritual element can be defined through heart wisdom in many ways. It can be the way a person looks right through us, into our very souls. It can be in the way they speak, both in words and mannerisms. It can be in their vision of life and mystery. It can be in the way they wear their sense of humor or hold their cup of coffee. And it can be in the way that their smile brings us a sense of comfort and well-being.

- Charlie Wehrley

JUST BEING

Wu wei is the ancient Chinese term for pure Being – literally non-doing. There is a flow to life and nature - and much of the time we humans ourselves as outside of it. Where we once were in the flow of life with other Earth creatures, our intellect, and self-awareness led us to eat that apple and step out of this flow. We try too hard, we push and drive and "should" on ourselves. We become human **doings** rather than human beings.

I don't know anyone who has found a permanent way back into the bliss of complete natural flow, but if we learn to **let go** and flow we can at least visit!

How do we lose our natural being? A good way to think of the process of recovering our ability to **be** is to imagine we are tightrope walkers making our way across an expanse. Things are going fine as long as we **fully give ourselves** to the process of walking the tightrope. But then it occurs to us to look down and that is when the trouble starts! We notice how high up we are and begin to question "What if I fall?" We have just taken a bite of the apple of self-consciousness – and we fall.

De-focus. Don't analyze your situation. Get out of your thoughts **and** your feelings – **just be aware**. Don't stare at yourself - find your thread of natural, spontaneous energy and follow it. All you have to do is loosen up and you will gradually find your flow – your river of being. It is always there waiting for you to dive into it. We can rejoin, at least to a degree and for a time, the other living creatures on this Earth who are just being without the blocks, barriers and stutters of self-consciousness. It is our birthright to BE.

- Christian R. Komor

LIFE IN THE FLOW

Living life in the flow requires being focused in the NOW by letting go of our need to control life. Control and flow are opposites. Control hinders the natural flow of life. Going with the flow means accepting that everything in my past is as it should be. Looking back, I may believe much of my past is a mess, but all of its messiness was necessary to make me who I am today. Going with the flow also means that our present, with all of its imperfection, is as it should be. And it means trusting that our future will unfold in its own perfectly imperfect way as it flows with the universal plan. All I have to do is get out of the way and relax into life.

Today make the conscious choice to get out of the way. Stop playing God. Relax, unwind, and go with the flow of God's universal plan. You will begin to see that everything is just as it should be. Life is not about how we want it to be. Life is about how everything actually is, despite our objections. People are who they are; the weather is as it is, and the day begins and flows as the universe flows. We are small, but important parts of that flow, and I need to be open to moving with the universal flow. When we just "are", everything is just as it should be. Awareness is the key to getting out of the way of both ourselves and the universal flow. Conscious surrender and release of my inner demands is the next step. And acceptance that life is exactly as it should be—moment by moment—rounds out our active choice to live life as it is.

- Charlie Wehrley

WEATHER

When you sail across an ocean, you submit to circumstances over which you have no control. Even shore side I don't control a lot of the big stuff. Not the disease waiting to awake in my genes. Not others, unless they are very unhealthy or under the age of ten. A lot happens outside of my sphere of influence. Is this uncontrolled Universe out to destroy me or to grow me? How I answer determines the climate in which I live.

– John R. Otterbacher

THE HERD WENT THAT-A-WAY!

"Keep close to nature's heart…and break clear away, once in a while. Climb a mountain or spend a week in the woods. Wash your spirit clean." – John Muir

Perhaps the most dangerous trait that we humans possess is that of the "herd mentality". Like animals seeking safety in numbers, we conform to what we perceive to be the behavior accepted by most of those of around us. History and behavioral science are filled with horrific examples of just how far herd mentality can take us into collective acts of destructive behavior – all the way to genocide.

The most profound recent example in our collective memory is the holocaust of World War II when vast numbers of citizens were willing to passionately follow their leadership off of a very high cliff with disastrous consequence. In hindsight we ask, "How could this happen!?" But herd behavior is very common – so common that few of us avoid it entirely in our lifetimes. The herd instinct is what leads us to racist behaviors, to bully other children, to segregate our fellow humans into "us" versus "them" groups, to follow a religious or political leader even when others are being hurt and our own values violated.

On the other hand, history shows us examples of brave individuals and groups who held to their principles and training in spite of a surging tide of agreement against them. We can determine to think for themselves and their rationality and self-respect leads them to take a different stand than those blindly following the human herd. Though we learn to mask it better as adults, saying "No," in the face of social pressure, is as difficult for us as it is for our young. The ability to remain rational, principled, and self-determined is a challenge we all face in large and small ways each day.
– Christian R. Komor

HAPPINESS

*H*appiness begins with me. I have power over my own life and I make choices that determine my personal happiness, or personal misery. The key to my happiness is within me; it is as simple and as difficult as self-acceptance: If I am happy with myself, I am happy with life. I am complete in myself and all of life compliments my completeness and happiness. No person or thing, no accomplishment or event makes me happy. They all compliment my happiness. I cannot be happy, however, If I am not happy with myself.

*S*o I go within the treasure box of my awareness to find acceptance for me, then maybe I can even start to love the real me. Maybe I am wonderfully made! Maybe I am as likable as people say I am! Maybe I am fun to be around! Maybe I am more handsome than I thought! And more talented! Maybe my spirit really can sing with a joy that's always been deep within me, buried under self-loathing.

*T*oday I take responsibility for my own happiness. I will go inside myself and open the treasure box that is me! I will not judge anything I find as good or bad; I will simply accept and learn to love myself just as I was knitted in my mother's womb and happiness gradually will be mine.

- Charlie Wehrley

SPIRITUAL NAKEDNESS

*When we stop defining ourselves with the thoughts/words we have imposed on ourselves, who we **think** we are disappears and we are free to simply be. All we have to do is observe by being present to ourselves and to the world around us, without any preconceived thoughts or judgments. Suddenly, it's as if we were just born into this life. Everything is fresh and new and we are at peace. We can choose to be open to ourselves and others. We can choose to be kind and affirming with ourselves and others.*

We must start with ourselves. Without making any harsh judgments, without comparing ourselves to anyone else, we need to become acquainted with our real selves for the first time. In doing so, we need to see the God-given beauty we each possess. If someone else's old words we once used to define ourselves creep up in our heads, we need to gently dismiss them. They are simply a shadow. Allow them to disappear under the light of your new affirming self-definition. It's this journey into the warmth of the great all-embracing Light and Love that enables us to open up and be vulnerable enough to know ourselves and to share ourselves with each other. For when we share ourselves mutually with one another on the deepest of spiritual levels, we experience the sanctity of witnessing, caressing, and affirming each other's souls.

If you want to be supremely happy in this life you have to know yourself—and love yourself—from inside-out. You have to journey to the center of your soul and love all that you find there. You have to allow your Higher Power to fully love you and then you have to be willing to face your fears of vulnerability, to walk through those fears, and to go for that deep spiritual soul-sharing connection with others. At that point you will face your greatest challenge of all: Allowing others to love you in all your spiritual nakedness.

- Charlie Wehrley

FAITH

Perhaps we control what matters least. We grasp, grapple and manage the smallest events – pay the mortgage and change the oil – draping ourselves in the illusion of security, even as someone loves us or ceases to, the truck meanders across the centerline, cancer percolates to life in a child. What do I believe? Is the Universe out to destroy me or grow me?

– John R. Otterbacher

LOOK AT ME

"And the heart that is soonest awake to the flowers is always the first to be touch'd by the thorns." - Thomas Moore

We all live in a time of "look at me!" The shrinking planet and its increased connectivity through many forms of media have launched a frenzy for attention. Talk shows, talking heads, "celebrities", paparazzi on every street corner - all of us jumping up and down hoping to be noticed, hoping someone, anyone will see we are here. And often by the time we are filtered through all the distortion and materialism, what others see of us is nothing like that which we really are. They see merely a construct of us, a shadow on a cave wall.

It seems to be a basic human need to be "seen"- to be witnessed in the play of life. Perhaps that is how this game was arranged – spirits in material form longing to be recognized by our fellows. There is nothing wrong with the human need to be seen, but we seem to have forgotten the immense power and grace in **seeing**. To witness **another**, to really see **them** without the distortions of who we wish they were or need them to be! To accept them for who they are and for who they are not – this is love.

So can we ask a different question? Instead of "How can I get people to see me, to listen to me, to know me ask "How can I listen better, learn more, discover those around me, accept them – love them?!" Transform our prayer "please see me" into "please help me to see." If we could all be so courageous we could turn our world inside out!

– Christian R. Komor

YOUR TRUE IDENTITY

Today and every day, take time to sit with yourself. Clear your mind of preconceived thoughts by observing yourself and everything around you. Allow yourself to simply be and allow old negative self-defining thoughts to disappear under the wonderment of your simply being content in the present moment.

Then take some time to allow positive self-defining thoughts to caress you into feeling the true beauty of who you are. Take back your power from those you have allowed to define you all of your past life. Become your own person. Own the beauty of your true identity as God intended when He breathed you into existence.

- Charlie Wehrley

BEYOND FEAR

*There is nothing dishonorable about fear. We come by our fears honestly, often in circumstances over which we have little control. There is a difference however between acknowledging fear and letting it run my life. Whatever my fears, I get to choose how I **behave**. I can live out beyond the contraction fear demands; stay radically open to others and to life itself. I get to choose!*

– John R. Otterbacher

BECOMING WHO YOU ARE

Becoming who you are… What could be more beautiful? It's a rewarding journey. And it lasts a lifetime. So it's important to enjoy the journey by being in touch with those moments of clarity when your awareness supplants the noise of your thoughts.

The journey begins by connecting with yourself inside; by becoming aware of what you are feeling in this moment and allowing your awareness to connect you with the Spirit that dwells within you. Each awareness provides a moment of clarity, a new perspective on the smallest aspects of who you are and the most mundane routines of your day.

The key to the brilliance of human life: The great ability we humans have to reflect upon and know ourselves, to connect with the Spirit inside of us and to follow the Light that emanates from within our souls. This moment of awareness can provide your soul with a rainbow that grounds you in the beauty of all things—in particular, the true beauty of your being.

- Charlie Wehrley

BENEITH THE SKIN

*I*magine that you have an hour to live and that you are lucid and pain free. Relive your life. Pay special attention to those memories which make you smile. These are the things that nourish you. In my life, they all have skin on - the people I love.

*A*nd so the essential question, to what extent is my daily life – my time and attention – devoted to those people who matter most to me, most nourish me?"

- John R. Otterbacher

ACTION AND CONTEMPLATION

Although I pay lip service to the value of both action and contemplation, I log more time on the action side of the ledger. It's time to restore balance. So I lie silent, still, looking up through the trees to the moon.

My essential heart is now beyond medical science to repair. I am aware that I must choose to live, choose and choose again. I will die otherwise. I must meet my possibilities halfway, must will to live, at least enough to offset the terrible force field into which I have slipped. Saddened at what has been lost, I must choose. In pain, or terrified, I must choose. I will live, in whatever shambled state I am left. My children will not grow up alone.

– John R. Otterbacher

REFINING A LIFE

We are pearls; however, gritty and rough we sometimes appear to be. The conflicts and pressures of our lives are the sandpaper necessary to smooth out these rough edges. When we truly embrace ourselves we can't help but embrace the world – accepting its pain and beauty as a natural expression of the light and vision that we have within.

– Thomas F. Crum

A HEART WIDE OPEN

The only way to live life is with your heart wide open. This is the only way that you fully experience the rain, sunshine, colors, textures and flavors of life. It's also the only way you really hear the soundtrack to your life.

A heart wide open brings the fullness of life to the surface of your every moment; your every breath; your every dream. And a heart wide open helps you to love all that you are, all that life is, all that other people are, and all that God is. A heart wide open allows you to shoot for the moon every day, and on those days when you miss the moon, it helps you to remember that you still have the stars.

- Charlie Wehrley

APPROVAL

If, like so many of us, you often find yourself relying on the approval of others, if you believe you need others to decide for you whether or not you are OK, then remember this. You already have the approval of your Maker! The only other approval you need is your own. Take back your power by approving of yourself. It's no one else's responsibility to decide if you are OK or not.

No one has the power to criticize you, or belittle you as "not good enough" unless you give them that power. Seek your own approval, claim your own values, stand for what you believe in, choose what you like, walk like you are comfortable in your shoes and people will be attracted to you-- the ones who count. The others create their own inner-hell by constantly judging and criticizing everyone. Cut yourself free so you can breathe naturally and stand on your own two feet proudly.

- Charlie Wehrley

WHY NOT?

Why not truly jump – leap fully into life, giving your-self to the world? Why hold back? Frustration turns to fascination and upset into growth. More and more you will find yourself exactly where you want to be – your work play and your play work.

We are designed to flow with the energy of our lives, but so often we resist that flow. In doing so we end up living half of a life and having half the fun. Find your flow and you will reward both yourself and everyone who you encounter!

- Thomas F. Crum

UNIVERSAL FLOW

Everything in the universe has a natural flow. We are part of that flow. Like every other element or living thing within the universe, we have our intended place and purpose. So then why is it that we humans spend more time struggling with life than we do flowing with it? We often make our day, and life, a struggle. It doesn't have to be.

We can take conscious, positive control of our day and we can ask our Higher Power to govern our subconscious input each day. Each morning, pray to your Higher Power and ask for the guidance to flow with the universe. Pray that God will keep you naturally within your place and focused on your purpose for each given day. Let go, stop struggling, and allow yourself to flow.

- Charlie Wehrley

DETACHMENT

Detachment is a form of surrender. Detachment is letting go of our need to have someone or something outside of ourselves make us OK. It's accepting and loving ourselves and our place in life. It's going with the flow of life while loving ourselves through it. It's allowing God to be God, life to be life, people to be people, and us to simply be us. We finally realize and accept that we can't control life or other people; and, with the help of our Higher Power, we gradually begin to let go.

We need to be the ones who end our inner-neediness through self-love and appreciation. First, we let go of our misconceptions concerning the amount of power we thought we had over other people. Second, we learn to detach from our addictions to certain "things."

Once we are able to start loving, accepting and appreciating ourselves, the holes in our souls will begin to close up and heal. The need to hold on to someone or something will subside and we will be able to let go and detach from having to possess power over others.

We will arrive at a healthy, peaceful place where all is well because we no longer need to strive or attach ourselves to others in order to be happy.

- Charlie Wehrley

DANCING ON A SHIFTING CARPET

Instead of seeing the rug as being pulled out from under us, we can learn to dance on a shifting carpet. The stumbling blocks of the past become the stepping stones to the future. The walls and boundaries of old can offer magical vistas as we move beyond them to new dances heretofore undiscovered, undreamed.

– *Thomas F. Crum*

GHOST FOOTPRINTS AND BREADCRUMBS

"The mind can make substance, and people planets of its own with beings brighter than have been, and give a breath to forms which can outlive all flesh." - Lord Byron

When you focus inside yourself you are as likely to find illusion as truth. You cannot control what thoughts pop into your head. You can control what happens next. Thoughts are just thoughts. Life is not our thoughts. We never experience life as it truly is. The world is always being filtered through our thoughts and conceptions.

To see through the illusions of life pause, stay still and allow yourself to look back on all the misinformation your mind has given you in the past – see through the illusion of your thoughts. Thoughts are not promises, agreements, predictions, foreshadowing, wishes, making a reservation, casting a shadow, or anything else – no matter how it seems or feels. Thoughts can be creative or dull, constructive or destructive but they are only thoughts. Sometimes our thought "weather" will be smooth and sometimes rough. But ultimately it is giving the thought importance that causes problems.

Take time to settle, center – find your bare awareness or what Zen Masters call bare attention. Being fully present to this moment takes you out of your thoughts. To do this focus hard on the details of your surroundings – there you will find reality - and see life clearly for what it is.

– Christian R. Komor

CAN A ROSE HAVE A BAD PETAL DAY?

Today cosmetic surgery is quite common across mainstream society. More and more people are concerned about facial-sagging when, in fact, what they should really be concerned about is soul-sagging. Beauty comes from within. Seems many of us would be better off looking inside ourselves to see where we need some spiritual tucks and tweaks. A simple look at nature, flowers in particular, helps us understand that authentic beauty blooms from inside-out. It's easy to see the beauty of a sunrise as light-beams paint red, orange and purple hues across a dark blue morning sky. And it's easy to see the beauty of wild flowers dancing across a summer field.

But do we take time to realize that this beauty begins within? Do we ever think of how nature loves itself from the inside-out? Probably not. Or do we think about how nature accepts each day as it unfolds through God's grace? We could learn powerful lessons from watching a rose. It accepts wild April winds blowing through its petals in the same gracious manner that it accepts lightly refreshing June winds.

So I ask you: Can a rose have a bad petal day? Can a daisy frown upon itself for not being "good enough?" Does the moon groan at its crescent face? No way! Nature doesn't see flaws in itself, or in the flow of daily life. Roses, daisies and the moon simply long to grow into the fullness of their beauty, and so all of nature nurture's itself toward that goal. Perhaps it is time to notice the unfolding beauty in our selves!

- Charlie Wehrley

A SPIRITUAL SPA

*H*ow often do we keep ourselves from growing into the fullness of our beauty by criticizing ourselves or our day as it unfolds? Probably too often. Everybody needs a spiritual spa day. We all need a day where we can drink-in the morning sunshine, cool off with afternoon breeze and relax in the warm waters of a refreshing evening shower. We could also use some quiet time with God and some spiritual lessons on saying loving words, instead of mean ones, to ourselves. And we could use a little time with loved ones-- allowing ourselves to feel lovable and loved.

*E*ssential beauty emanates from within our souls and it transforms our personalities into peaceful radiance and our bodies into glowing temples of the Spirit.

– Charlie Wehrley

DIE TO WHO YOU THINK YOU ARE

Let go of who you think you are, the form, thoughts, identity, intensity, longing, roles, flesh and bone. Let go of everything that seems to be you, and experience who you really are. The energy that lends itself to form, but is not form. The spirit that pounds within your heart, but throbs as well in the ocean swells, in the fish and birds, which pulses in the sun and wind.

Can you die enough to who you think you are to experience who you really are? Can you?

– John R. Otterbacher

LIVING OUR OWN LIFE

*L*iving a harmonious life, one in which you maintain an overall sense of well-being, is as simple as "live and let live." In other words, own the power that is yours and let go of your need to usurp power that is not yours to own. If you love yourself enough to own your personal power, to set proper boundaries with others, to love and treat yourself with kindness, to respect yourself by speaking up for your needs and honoring yourself, then you will be half way to happiness.

*L*ikewise, if you love others enough to allow them to own their personal power, to set their own boundaries, to allow them to be who they are and not who you want them to be, if you treat them with love, kindness and proper respect, then your happiness—and theirs—will be complete. Maintaining an over-all sense of well-being is as simple—and as difficult—as that. Own your power and allow others to own theirs. It really boils down to being a good steward of your life by practicing proper self-care and allowing others to do the same.

- Charlie Wehrley

LIVE SIMPLY

We live better on less. We live better when we live frugally. The trade off - experience for acquisition. Even as our material acquisitions diminish, the primacy of our relationships becomes more obvious. Saving becomes a game - fun to some extent.

Letting go of possessions can be bittersweet, life-altering, and exhilarating. Working on it together, equal parts discipline and dream, strengthens our connection

In these years aboard the good boat Grace I have stepped back from everything but my family and the good boat Grace. A latter day Henry Miller, I have nothing. I am the happiest man alive.

– John R. Otterbacher

BE THE WONDER

Humans are such an interesting lot. Over time, even our wildest dreams can become realities. Consider flying. Since the earliest times we have longed to soar with the birds, looking down on the world from a place of heavenly freedom. Today we can soar and glide and swoop with the best of our fine-feathered friends.

Yet having realized our grandest of dreams we immediately forget to enjoy them. We turn the glory of flight into just one more modern convenience, forgetting to even look out the window as we pass over untold beauty beneath us.

What will happen in your amazing world today? Don't miss a minute of the ride!

— *Thomas F. Crum*

FEEDING THE GOOD DOG

"Nothing in the affairs of men is worthy of great anxiety." - *Plato*

An Indian American sage once remarked, "We all have within us a "good dog" and a "bad dog." The one we feed is the one that becomes the strongest. The other grows weak and fades away." Yet how much time do we spend focusing on our dark side, our "bad dog" – resisting and fighting it? We only succeed in perfecting its viciousness.

Whatever your bad dog is, don't feed the dog and it will grow weaker. Instead focus on and feed the good dog within you! Let go of shame and self-recrimination for what is past. Make amends, if needed, and focus forward on what needs to be <u>right</u>! Think, if you spent as much energy on your strengths as your weaknesses, how amazing life could be. On second thought, don't just think about it – DO IT!

Often our mind tends to puts a negative spin on events and our role in them. We focus on what we believe is wrong with us, on all our many mistakes and failings. We imagine that we can see into the future and know the ultimate outcome of those actions by which we judge ourselves so harshly for. We cannot know the outcome!! What appears a mistake or misfortune today may have a wondrous purpose we cannot fathom! Perhaps someone needed to learn from our example and will be saved great turmoil and torment. The wisest course is not to judge – anything or anyone……EVER.

– *Christian R. Komor*

THE PRODIGAL GOD

*G*od wants us to be honest, but we have to first be honest with ourselves in order to be honest with God. We have to be ready for God to show up. God is always present for us, but God will not enter into a serious relationship with us until we are ready—ready to be open, truthful, responsible, and fully open to our real selves and not false idols.

*S*o who is the real God? The Prodigal God! God is the parent who loves us unconditionally, despite our flaws and failed behaviors. He loves our personalities, how we look (even without our clothes!), how we think, and how we move; He loves our dreams and desires, our light side and our dark side, our successes and our failures.

*F*ailures? Yes, even our failures. After all it takes a lot of courage to fail and to learn from our failures, to gather wisdom from failure and to move forward toward success. God loves everything about us. He may not always like our behavior, but certainly He's big enough to look beyond "bad" behavior and to love us even more when we're trapped in it. God's there to fully support us when we're lost and struggling, but we have to allow Him in by being fully honest with ourselves and thus God. Being fully honest with ourselves means believing that we are wonderfully made by God; few of us really believe this. Oh, we believe God made us, but we have a hard time swallowing the idea that we are "wonderfully" made. Sitting with God and being fully honest about how beautiful we are might make us cry—tears of sadness and tears of joy. We may feel deep, dark remorse over having believed bad things about ourselves for so long, and for failing to see our true beauty. Then, having grieved ourselves clean, we may experience tears of true joy at being amazed at how our faces have become things of beauty to us.

- Charlie Wehrley

WRESTLING WITH GOD

When we take the time to wrestle with the God of our understanding, like Jacob did; when we take the time to ask God questions, like Jesus instructed us to do; we will make great strides in our spiritual life. Jacob had no fear while wrestling with God and Jesus told us, "ask and you will receive" because asking is how we get answers. Many people think "ask and you will receive" means ask for the winning lottery numbers and you'll get them. That's not what Jesus had in mind. Asking and receiving is all about gaining knowledge and spiritual, life-changing wisdom.

In order to receive this knowledge and wisdom, however, we have to be willing to be fully transparent—open and honest—with God. We have to express our true thoughts, desires and feelings; and be 100 percent open to giving and receiving in our relationship with God. This also means that we have to accept the answers that come to us, even if we don't like them initially. Answers that we resist are answers we need to probe deeper in to understanding. Feelings of resistance are signs that we are being challenged in the very areas of our lives that we most need new mental/emotional/spiritual growth.

So wrestle with God. Don't be a weenie. God is big enough to take anything we dish out. And God will be honest with us as long as we are willing to be honest with God. All we have to do is open the door and truthfully allow God into our lives.

- Charlie Wehrley

EVOLUTION AND CONNECTION

All species go through a crisis point of evolution in which they move toward a more interdependent, harmonious relationship with their environment. This shift is what ensures their survival. It is an evolutionary centering – nature's way of moving us from separateness to connectedness.

Instead of contracting in an ever-tightening spiral of defensiveness, we can choose to expand in an ever-growing circle of cooperation and understanding. From this centered place we have the courage to embrace conflict knowing that it is a splendid opportunity to choose a future of growth and prosperity.

— *Thomas F. Crum*

LETTING GO OF SHAME

No one is inherently bad and **shame** is never appropriate. Anyone who claims that a certain person is inherently bad is guilty of dehumanizing that person. Everyone is created in the image and likeness of God, and as a result, everyone is inherently good. Our behavior is sometimes bad, and we have the emotion of **guilt** to help us correct that bad behavior and to make amends.

A little guilt is good for the soul; but shame is never good. No one should ever feel shame at being who they are. If we feel shame about ourselves-- be it our gender, body, sexual-orientation, ethnicity, physical characteristics or personality—we need to surrender that shame to our Higher Power and ask for help in overcoming our shame.

God sees nothing shameful about the way He created each of us, and so there's no reason why any of us should feel shame about being who we are. Learn from the guilt to be a better person and surrender the shame to God. Set yourself free and allow your soul to shine!

- Charlie Wehrley

ORIGINAL SIN

*T*he neurological equivalent of Original Sin is the binary brain's innate tendency to divide reality into discreet parts – here/there, now/then, body/soul, man/environment, and human/Divine. What it can't do in its tenacious duality is experience the unity everything has with everything else, the unity of body and soul and nature and Spirit – the One without other, the Only All.

*T*his is the realm of that mystics accessed most often in profound stillness. In stillness we can find at least some measure of the Garden of Eden again inside ourselves. We can repatriate ourselves with Being.

– *John R. Otterbacher*

YOU ARE A WORK OF ART

*W*hat would it be like if we lived our lives as works of art in progress? What would it be like if we could live joyfully in every moment, absorbing the magic and freshness of each new day without hurry? What would it be like if each breath and each action were part of an unfolding masterpiece, a continued process of artistry!

*B*ring forth a life of power, freedom, and joy! Use pressure, change and the unknown as an artist would – sculpt the masterpiece of your life! Breathe and extend your life energy so that you become larger than the struggling personality called "Me." You are in reality much larger, more vast, and far more deeply connected. Let your spaciousness look lovingly down on this form and know that you are simply on a journey back home.

*S*tay unattached, observant, and present to the struggle - all the while knowing that it's all an illusion of mind and all illusions are transitory. You can watch the movie knowing it's only that and in your own way can change your mind-set about it at any time. It is all part of the rich adventure that is life.

— *Thomas F. Crum*

ACCEPTING THE DARK SIDE

*L*ife isn't about rewards; it's about being who you are. But if you still want a really great reward in life - Be who you are and allow other people to be who they are. There's no greater reward for we humans than being exactly who God made each of us to be. Stop existing in the hollow shell of who you "should" be. Many people are stuck there and they spend a lifetime inside the false shell of "should be".

*T*his shell requires that you **deny your dark side**. Family, society, and church created this shell (remove the "s" and notice that the word becomes "hell"). They decided who you "should" be. Then they told you how to act, what to wear, what to say, what to believe, who to trust, etc.

*A*s adults, we have to grow beyond this (s)hell. We have to take responsibility for our lives. We have to decide what's acceptable and what's not acceptable—for us. This means we need to work at **accepting our dark sides** by bringing them into some sort of balance with our light sides. Balance requires that we explore and embrace our dark sides; learn from them all they have to teach us about the "real" us and then take that knowledge and integrate it into our being.

*E*xpress your "true" self. Let the rest of the world go on spinning as it chooses. It's better to know who loves you for the "real" you. And it's better to know it NOW. Those who loved the "fake" (but perfect) you may attempt to guilt and shame you into going back inside your (s)hell, but that's OK. Allow them to go on being forever "fake" with someone else. The real loss will be theirs, not yours. Embrace your dark and light sides. Find balance. Be all sides of yourself. And be them now.

- Charlie Wehrley

THIS SWEET MOMENT

"Imagine there's no Heaven. It's easy if you try. No hell below us, above us only sky. Imagine all the people living for today." - John Lennon

I am not an atheist. I do believe in God and a future beyond this current existence that you and I share. But, in a way I think the world might be a better place if we knew that this was our only shot at making ourselves and others save, loved and happy. In fact I try to forget about the "ever after", or the next life, or the pearly gates or whatever may lie in that "undiscovered country". I am here now in whatever circumstances I happen to be in and this is where I can either contribute to, or take away from my welfare and that of those around me.

There is a flow to life and nature - and much of the time we humans are outside of it. Where we once were **in** the flow of life with other Earth creatures, our intellect, and self-awareness led us to eat that apple and step **out** of this flow. How did we lose our natural being? Imagine a tightrope walker making her way across an expanse (wishing to herself that her tights would stop creeping up). Things are going fine as long as she continues to **give herself fully** to the process of walking the tightrope. But then the darn pink tights take a sudden creep upward and our intrepid tightrope walker is abruptly distracted - and it occurs to her to look down. That's when the trouble starts! She notices how high up she is, and then starts thinking about how she is really not getting paid very much and can't even qualify for tips! She starts to questions what she is there for, what she is doing with her life and, of course "What if I fall?" She has just taken a bite of the apple of **self-consciousness** – and she falls.

*T*he moral of this story? Well, there's the obvious lesson - especially for you guys out there – about not wearing pink leotards that are too tight! But there is also a deeper lesson – live the present moment. Some might even say that is how we got kicked out of the Garden of Eden. We lost our ability to BE in the present and started thinking.

*W*hat if there is a Heaven? What if there is a Hell? What if we are reincarnated over and over? What if we dissolve into and become one with the great mass of energy that is the Universe? What if our neurons turn off and that's just it - nothingness - no conscious awareness? Now we can have faith in one scenario or the other, but honestly we just don't know except by "faith". We just don't know so the only thing that makes sense is to assume THIS JUST MIGHT BE OUR ONE BIG CHANCE! This might be our one shot to love and be loved - to care and be cared for. Regardless, it's a good investment to learn to be here NOW. Don't analyze your situation. Get out of your thoughts **and your feelings** – just **be aware**. Find your thread of natural, spontaneous energy and follow it. All you have to do is loosen up and you will gradually find your flow – your "river of being". It is always there waiting for you to dive into it. It is our birthright to BE.

*T*he challenge is to really live in the awareness of how precious and wonderful life is. We are talking about being TRULY alive, not the shuffling zombie-like existences many of us experience. Truly ALIVE! So alive that our exuberance - our pure desire for life - is unmistakable to others. Our aliveness is informed and empowered by the awareness of the **possible finality** of life. There is a certain amount of time from cradle to grave. In between are all these incredibly special people and experiences. Such awareness is overwhelmingly sweet and powerful.

*I*t is easy to be overwhelmed with the sacredness and intensity of being truly alive. So easy to give in to the fear of really celebrating – fear of really saying "my life is now!" How strange to be afraid of what most of us would say we long for the most. How *different our world might be if not for the fear of aliveness. At an interfaith prayer vigil in Newtown, Connecticut following the school shooting there, our President observed that "the world's religions — so many of them represented here today — start with a simple question: Why are we here? What gives our life meaning?" We may never know. What we do know is that in **this** life in **every** moment and **every** choice we can either be part of the **problem** or part of the **solution**. Yes, **dream** of the "undiscovered country", but **live** as if this life is your only light and will one day be gone.*

- Christian R. Komor

RIGHT IS RIGHT

People are people. Rules are rules. Love is love. Right is right. So why can't we human beings get along in this world? We need to accept that people are people, just like we are; that everyone is different to some degree, but that different isn't bad; and we need to stop judging other people's behavior when we have no ability to read their hearts. It's too easy to judge people's behavior when we haven't walked in their shoes; when we really know nothing about their struggles or brokenness; and when, genetically and personally, we are all so different. Jesus didn't judge those who had been condemned as "dregs" of society. He loved them, embraced them, and healed them.

We are called to do the same. We are called to love, accept, embrace, and heal those around us. And we start by not judging them, and by not using them as a means of gaining approval from the self-righteous. As Christ said, the self-righteous already have their reward in this life. They need a reward, we don't. Let's live by the law of love and do the right thing simply because it is right and just. Rewards aren't necessary. Doing right for the sake of rightness is all we need to allow our souls to shine

- Charlie Wehrley

RUNNING ON SPIRITUAL EMPTY

We are often so frantically in motion that it never even occurs to us to take time in our day to feed our soul. And we seldom realize that we need to feed our soul in the same way we need to feed our body until the day comes when we mentally, emotionally, spiritually and physically collapse. Running on spiritual empty has become the way of the world. But what many people don't understand is that feeding your spiritual life is first and foremost essential to feeding every other aspect of your life. When we take the time to breathe and spiritually nourish ourselves from within, we clear our heads of deafening clatter.

We can also relax our bodies. We can slump into a bath tub filled with bubbles and simply be, simply enjoy. It may then occur to us afterwards that maybe we'd like some steamed vegetables and warm, fresh bread for once; or a little wine and some strawberries. After we finish eating, endorphins are dancing through our heads and so we decide that a quiet walk with some gentle, peaceful music playing on our MP3 player would be nice. It gives us time to think about some of the things we need to surrender to our Higher Power and to process some of the difficult feelings we've been avoiding while, at the same time, boosting our energy. On returning home, we take some time to journal about all that we've just experienced; mentally, emotionally, physically and spiritually—all because we took some much needed soul-time for ourselves. We can now sleep with a fairly clean slate and wake up refreshed in the morning. Make an appointment with yourself to take a soul break.

-Charlie Wehrley

THE SACRED NATURE OF ADVENTURE

"You can break my heart and I ain't going to run. I don't scare easy for no one"
– Tom Petty

Unlike Tom Petty, all of us have things in life that scare us. If you think you are fearless it simply means you haven't run into any of your really scary stuff yet. It's waiting for you – don't worry. No one with a functioning brain is fearless.

Now you may indeed be brave! Bravery is like confidence mixed with a strong measure of fortitude. All we need in order to have bravery is the willingness to begin. To be willing to step into the fray – to enter the forest even at its darkest point where there is no path.

When we carry our bravery into a situation we fear (and live through it) we get **courage**. You don't get courage before you do the thing you fear – you get it after. Courage is the willingness to keep going once things get unpleasant. To keep going even when really scary stuff is bursting all around us, reaching up through the earth with twisted claws, grabbing at our ankles, weighting down on us like a heavy cloud bank filled with lightening. Courage is what keeps you keep going after your dang foolish bravery gets you into some nasty situation. Like bravery courage is a process, not an end-product. You are still in "the suck" during the courage phase.

Generally on the other side of courage is wisdom. Wisdom is the byproduct of facing what you fear – whether you face it inside your mind, or in the world outside your mind. (Sometimes the two are hard to separate.) So bravery and courage are elements in a process which leads to wisdom.

Wisdom invariably is the awareness of the temporary nature of everything. Remember how our fears are based on imagined outcomes (poverty, illness, loss, death)? Well, on the other side of the bravery-courage process is an amazing realization. Everything is temporary. Most importantly you are temporary – or at least you as you know yourself now. And if everything is temporary including you then everything you experience is simply an adventure. That realization is wisdom!

Now we can talk about all this out in the open because you have already been through the bravery-courage-wisdom process haven't you? Sure, by the time you read articles like this you know you have - probably more than once.

So what makes a thing scary? Generally it is the outcome. We are afraid to drive on the highway because we fear we might lose control and crash. We are afraid to lose our job because we might go hungry. We are afraid to swim across the lake because we are afraid we might drown. (Well, some of us are afraid there might be monsters at the bottom of the lake, but I mean normal people.) We are afraid to die because we might not like what happens afterward.

Life becomes about adventures and the end days of a life well-lived are filled with stories of adventures. Indeed, stories are one measure of a life. Stories of our adventures are a very sacred thing. We bravely or foolishly got ourselves into something that required courage to traverse and resulted in wisdom – a lightening of our death-grip on life……..an inspiring, freeing, refreshing awareness of our mortality.

- Christian R. Komor

THE FOUNTAIN OF YOUTH

"All that's sacred comes from youth." - Eddie Vedder

Young adults - those brave souls fresh from High School and off to make their way in a brand new world - are such a sweet, special age group. Like young deer they are venturing out from their parents protective watch, tentative and yet bold all at the same time. Each and every one with something they will bring to the world and so many exciting things to discover about themselves.

It's a very exciting, magical time, but it also **seems** to be a very sad, fleeting one. Here one is old enough to drive and stay out late and fall in love and everything - but tomorrow, we may be putting on a suit and tie every day, paying bills, sitting at a desk. It's **seems** like we only get a tiny window to learn who we really are as mature people, before the burden of modern life crushes who we wished to become.

"And we don't know
Just where our bones will rest to dust
I guess forgotten and absorbed
Into the earth below"
"And we don't even care
as restless as we are"

But the **truth** is you're never too old for love, and adventure, and rebellion, and change. Sure, you may not look as cool doing it with grey hair, but **do it anyway** - no matter what holds you back. Stay out with your friends until 4 AM, tell the person you love that you love them, see the world, tell people who are trying to keep in you in "your place" so you can "act your age" to f**k off, listen to music that makes you happy to be alive, or okay with wishing you weren't. Don't even bother trying to "live outside the box" because there **aren't** any boxes except the ones we put over ourselves! And for goodness sake don't worry too much about the future, because tomorrow may never come, but **today** is here for sure.

Youth is not a time period so much as it is a state of mind – a permission we give ourselves to "be all we can be" and explore beyond the limits of what is possible. Live from the youth inside you – that fountain of energy, ideas, passions, and possibilities which all spill into the future and eventually into that undiscovered country. And when you finally arrive in **that** place make sure you bring your fountain of youth with you! I am pretty sure God will be delighted with the adventure you have made out of the gift of life and want to hear all about it!

- Christian R. Komor

SELF-LOVE

We will never know peace without unconditional self-acceptance. And unconditional self-acceptance is a natural byproduct of self-love. Until we gain unlimited self-love and acceptance, we will continue to be controlled by fear. Fear will remain our master. Fear will pull our strings and we will perpetually dance to its dirge of manipulation and control. We will hold tight to our false illusion of having power; power to get from others what we refuse to give to ourselves. And our love of this imaginary power to calculate, manipulate, and control others will continue to weave a path of self-destruction and emotional mutilation of everyone we set our sights on. It will never be a pathway to peace, happiness, or lasting love.

We can choose love of power, or we can choose the power of love. When we decide to choose the power of love, we will be freely assisted by our Higher Power. But we have to be willing to work with our Higher Power. We need to identify our areas of shame, guilt and regret about ourselves, our behavior and our past. And we need to honestly discuss them with God. We also need to be willing to completely let go of all of these negative roadblocks to self-love and acceptance. In other words, we have to be willing to surrender them to our Higher Power and to fully let them go into oblivion.

Then we need to make this our daily mantra: "When the power of love for myself and others is greater than the love of power to manipulate and control others, I will know peace." Eventually, hopefully, we'll be able to modify this statement to "because the power of love for myself and others is greater than my love of power to manipulate and control others, I now know peace."

-Charlie Wehrley

HEALING THE RIFT

Isn't it ironic that some celebrate fear as if it were a virtue? We are told to fear our bodies, fear the world, and fear eternal punishment for our mistakes and failings.

Why can't faith mean that I can let go of my tortured self-loathing in the awareness that - whatever my personal limitations – I am part of Something Much Larger. It is this larger life force from which everything I experience emerges, from which I cannot be apart?

- John R. Otterbacher

WILLING TO LET GO

Changing the world always starts with your willingness to let go of anything that keeps you stuck, from fear and apathy to solidified belief systems.

*To truly have good news, you must **be** the good news. When your life is a contribution, a source of value to the world, you are living beyond the gold, beyond success. The only limit to how far you can go is in your willingness to adventure into the unknown.*

— *Thomas F. Crum*

LET GO OF FEAR

There are many freedoms we'd all discover and immediately treasure if we could just let go of our fears about us. Paramount among our numerous fears is probably this one: "What will others think of me?" Paramount among our new beliefs needs to be: "Who gives a rat's ass what anyone else thinks of me!" We waste way too much energy and lose way too much of our natural lives being fearful of what other people think of us, and trying to remake ourselves over to be acceptable to people—many of whom we don't even know. If they think we're silly, well, good. We have the right to be silly. Better to be silly than to be "dead" with fear of expressing ourselves.

How about all those other fears we harbor? You know the ones about controlling every facet of life and everyone around us. Many of us are fearful of never being loved, changing jobs, losing a loved one, growing old (alone), difficult emotions, facing serious illness or death, difficult bosses or coworkers, money problems, marital issues or even getting out of bed in the morning. We become timid possessed by our worries. We don't really live life. We don't dance through life. We can create beauty in this life only through love. We never create beauty through fear.

So what's the answer? Conscious living! We need to be aware of the fears that darken our lives. We need to look at each of them carefully and decide to take our power back from them. And we **can do this** by connecting more frequently with our Higher Power and trusting more in divine providence. We also need to trust more in ourselves. We need to understand that when we make faith-based choices, instead of fear-based ones, there is **no guarantee** that everything will work out as we wanted, but that **everything will work out**. How much better your life would be if it were controlled by love and not fear. Your soul can shine when it is free of fear and filled with love.

– Charley Wehrley

DRIVING OURSELVES SANE

In the thousands of years we have been residents of the planet Earth, the human race has been graced by some amazing prophets, philosophers, wise men, religious teachers and yes, even self-help authors! If we have already received wisdom and instruction, both human and divine - if we have already received the answers that will allow us to lead happy and fulfilled lives on a peaceful and well cared for planet, then what's the problem? Where are the results!?

*The answer, I'm afraid, is actually so obvious it did not occur to me until my life was more than half over! PRACTICE!! Yup, the daily **application** of what healthy way of living and being until **we become good at it**! And what is the one thing that our multitasking, attention deficient, channel-flipping, modern culture is not designed to do? Practice! Now you're starting to see the problem!*

*So we must know **what to do** and we must actually **practice doing it** - but where and when is that well-informed practice going to happen in this busy, chaotic, hectic world? And how do we make that practice universal enough that it will have a global impact on the world around us?*

*There is only **one place** that can happen – and again it's so obvious it's shocking – the **one place** is that carbon-spewing, road-kill producing, ecological blight known as **the automobile**! Driving is the **only** activity that a large enough portion of the people (in the developed world anyway) do on a regular enough basis.*

Now, personally I wish it could happen somewhere more poetic like an ancient cathedral, a Tibetan yurt, a yoga studio, or a martial arts dojo high on a snowcapped mountain peak but our practice field needs to be one we are **compelled to visit almost daily**

*A*lso, and very importantly, the time we spend in our cars is a common ground on which members of modern society meet and exchange connection and communication. If we take the time to pay attention to that communication and the actions we choose while driving, we can move ourselves and our fellow travelers a little further each day toward a more supportive, positive, and caring social culture.

*M*ost of us would agree that honesty, integrity, and compassion are human traits that contribute to the benefit of human society. What if everyone (or even a nice big fat percentage of us) made a conscious effort to "pay it forward" and express those key values and virtues in our driving behavior – the most frequent and consistent interaction most of us have with other members of our communities? Think of the ripples made by a single pebble dropped into a pool of water. They radiate outward until they reach the edges of the pool. In this case, the "pool" is humankind and there is no limit to how far the ripples from a single action can go.

*S*uch a simple concept and yet there is no refuting the principle. Shifting our driving behaviors to incorporate and express positive values and virtues cannot help but change the world. It's a foregone conclusion! FINALLY we have all the elements we need – the knowledge, the will, and a vehicle for regular practice that will ALSO, by nature of its social aspects, radiate positive change out into society. Let's take a look at a couple of examples.

*A*ccident rates skyrocket in moments of indecision. We are heading to a yard sale and pass what we thought was the right street, but…well, we just aren't sure…was it "Starbust Lane" or "Starstruck Avenue?" BANG!! We have run into a van with a mother and her two children in the back seat. No one is injured – this time. We are far, far safer statistically when we know where we are going and have a map in our head of how to get there. Leaving the driveway with uncertainty is a recipe for disaster.

So we make a change in how we are driving, we learn to **plan ahead** using either our internalized "map" of where we live, an external map made of paper, or microchips. Along the way if our destination becomes unclear we stop, reassess, and then proceed once we are again certain. We can also extend our foresight out ahead of us as we drive, creating a cushion of space around our vehicle by leaving open space in front of our vehicle and avoiding driving in packs or other driver's blind spots. We have just demonstrated the power of **planning ahead** in our interactions with other drivers – making both ourselves and other drivers safer.

So now that we are practicing being clear about our destination and planning ahead while on the road, we take that practiced ability and transfer it to our personal life outside the car! We begin noticing that although we are making more than the average income we never seem to have money to take vacations or make major purchases. So we become proactive rather than reactive with our finances, **plan ahead** what we want to save for, and start putting away a piece of each paycheck for that financial destination. We observe that we seem to be dating the same sorts of people and it never seems to work out. So we take some time to **plan ahead** – looking more closely at what we really need in a relationship. We find we never have enough time for to play with our children in the evening so we start **planning ahead** to leave time available.

And so our practice in **planning ahead** while driving, has **transferred to choices we make in other areas of our personal life.** This then is the process of "Driving Ourselves Sane" (KEI Global, 2012)... Changing ourselves and our society with the automobile as classroom...Turning a dangerous, polluting machine into a vehicle for transformation.

- *Christian R. Komor*

TRUE WEALTH

One of the reasons I like living on a boat is that I live better when I live frugally. In a very real way I trade accumulation for experience; the intensity of fully experienced moments. Having less also ratchets up the importance of our relationship. We solve problems rather than trying to buy our way out of trouble.

Our wealth is how we feel about each other, what there is between us.

– John R. Otterbacher

THE HUMAN CONDITION

A young father I knew in his 30s died last Friday, leaving behind a wife and three small children. There are always questions in these types of situations: Why? Why someone so young? Why someone who had a wife and kids? The "why" questions can be endless and there's never a quantifiable answer. I don't believe in "it was just his time" or that God called him home. There's too much cruelty to these pat answers and they make God seem like a beast. What purpose could there be behind such imagined acts of God? I see no redeeming purpose to seizing a young man from his young family.

I do believe that life happens and that Earthly existence contains a measure of randomness.

*W*hen someone dies and there is no acceptable answer to "why," I believe it's simply the human condition. It's the way we're wired. It's random. God didn't plan it and God didn't decide to call anyone home in the prime of their life. God is there, though, to help us through the suffering of it all. God is the pillar, the energy boost we need to help us grieve the unexplainable loss we suffer when someone close to us dies. God provides the tears to heal us so that our souls can once again shine and we can move forward in life.

*I*f you are suffering from a great loss, allow yourself to grieve. Feel the pain, taste the tears, experience the love that is forever there for you, and know you can allow your soul to regain its rainbow.

- Charlie Wehrley

SACRED CONNECTION

We know from statistics that violence is actually reducing over time. There are fewer wars and the wars we are having claim less lives. What is on the increase is a type of disaffected violence - desperate acts by lost and outlying men and women. These are twisted and distorted creatures that were once just like us. They have had the misfortune, or wrong turns, that have led to a profound estrangement from all connection - to themselves, their fellows, and their community. They have drifted so far from the flock that even acts of mass killing to them seem sane.

*I learned early in my work as a psychologist in a maximum security prison that this type of disconnected, explosive violence does **not** happen when there **is connection**. In connection with our families and friends life will still present us with pain and suffering, but the fabric of those relationships keeps us from spinning wildly out of control. I learn the lesson again each time I encounter someone who is "different" and disenfranchised - **and I do nothing**, or avoid them. I know from my experience and training that right in front of me is a potential social disaster waiting to happen, yet I usually do not go to stand next to them, or try to break into their solitary, tortured world and try and make a connection.*

What holds me back? What holds you back? Fear I guess, and in giving in to that fear we fail the victims of the next school shooting, or subway bombing. Nothing excuses such acts, but if we truly care about these tragedies we must do what we can and it's human connection is what makes the difference. Every step we take as individuals to build social connection and return lone wolves to the fold is a step away from the next mass shooting. In spite of how uncomfortable it might be, we need to do our best to reach out to others even if they seem different. Human connection makes all the difference.

- Christian R. Komor

ACCEPTING OURSELVES

There are many people in our lives that we need to "forgive". The first one is us. No one has done a poorer job of loving and accepting us as we are than we have. As a result, we have cruelly criticized and victimized ourselves. We have spent a lifetime being ashamed of and angry with the person that we are-- simply because we could not be the person we wanted ourselves to be. It's time to wake up to reality. The person we wanted us to be is fantasy. The person that we are is reality. Fantasy is about perfection. Reality is about imperfection. Reality is about an imperfect world populated by imperfect people. We are one of those imperfect people and it's time we accepted it. As soon as we can accept our limitations and imperfections, we can begin to accept the person that we really are. The person who is beautiful despite his or her flaws; the person who is talented despite his or her mistakes; the person who is love personified despite his or her neediness; and the person that God created and loves despite his or her being "perfectly imperfect."

But it's pretty hard to love yourself at all when you have felt so unlovable your entire life. Loving ourselves "enough" requires facing all of those parts of ourselves that we find unacceptable. It requires acknowledging them and the fact that most of them are simply the human condition—something we all share in common. No one is exempt from the human condition and we are all pretty much equally as imperfect. Learning to empathize with our least desirable "parts," helps us to have compassion toward them and ourselves, in general. We are then able to be kinder to ourselves. And with that kindness we will find a sense of peacefulness. This peacefulness is acceptance. Practice loving yourself enough to accept the unacceptable.

- Charlie Wehrley

FEAR AND CONNECTION

"Lord, You know my many masks. They represent the fear, deep within my heart, that arises from unhealed hurts. Old negative self-beliefs cause me to feel "not good enough." When I feel this way, I am often afraid to voice my important wants and needs, even with those I love most. Help me, Lord, to act from that place of Perfect Love within my heart. Send your Light into my empty darkness. Help me to know and acknowledge my needs and desires in healthy, non-threatening ways with loved ones.

I trust that your loving guidance will keep us from being threatened by our differences. I will work at accepting that I don't have to agree with others in order to love them. I can agree to disagree without anyone having to be right or wrong, good or bad. Help me to open my heart to honest communication. Every authentic relationship is built on honesty, truth tempered by kindness and love. Help me to remove my masks and to be genuine with others. As I come to accept myself and others as we are, I will better be able to express my desires and needs. My neediness will subside and I will gradually live interdependently with others as we begin to complement each other. Today, I surrender my fears to You, Lord, so that You may mold my brokenness into a beautiful mosaic that honestly reflects Your image and likeness. Amen."

- Charlie Wehrley

ONE MOMENT

Do less and experience more. Constant motion can be both a denial of life and a protection from the immensity of even one moment fully experienced.

Life is richest when slowed down to that place where the elemental intensity takes over - the incandescence of a glance, a touch, a quality of light or dark, a leaf in the street. Can I be wide awake to the only moment I have? This... This...

– John R. Otterbacher

POWERLESS – NOT HELPLESS

Accepting that we are all so powerless in matters of life and death is very difficult. I think this is part of the reason we humans work so hard to keep ourselves and loved ones alive medically. But there's only so much any of us can do. Sooner or later, we have to let go and trust God. It's important to trust that God will guide us to what's best for us and those we love. It's hard to let go of the need to control outcomes, but it's necessary.

We can have no peace until we accept our limitations, accept the fact that we are so powerless over so much in life—and surrender them to God. It takes great faith to surrender, let go and trust that God will make all things right in the long run. But it's the only way to successfully live from day to day.

If you are struggling with something, be aware of any denial that is trying to hide or sugarcoat the truth. Accepting the truth, surrendering our loss of personal power to God and trusting that God will always do what's best is the true path to peace. Denial is a Band-Aid. Sooner or later we are challenged to accept reality and allow God's grace to carry us through our fears.

- Charlie Wehrley

AWARENESS

Awareness runs the world in that each of us -- saint and sinner alike – acts in accordance with his or her level of awareness. To change the world I must raise the level of awareness, starting with my own.

On what do I chose to focus? To what do I give my limited time and attention? How I answer will determine both the quality and the contribution of my life.

– John R. Otterbacher

DREAM AND DISCIPLINE

A dream without discipline is a fantasy. Lip service without action is lame at best, hypocrisy at worst. I claim to value both action and contemplation. Do I live that way?

Nobody is going to give me the time for solitude and reflection. Do I have the clarity and the discipline to carve the hours out of an unrelenting schedule for the nourishment only stillness provides?

– John R. Otterbacher

AT HOME WITH OUR SELF

Ever know someone who's comfortable in their humanness and simply carefree? You know the type of person I'm talking about. They don't care if the wind blows through their hair and messes it up, or if their jeans are slightly dirty, or if their behavior is a little naughty. If they're feeling lazy, they allow themselves to be. They laugh a lot at life and they glide along on their dreams because they aren't afraid to dream or to take risks. When they fail, they chalk it up to experience, pick themselves up, and move on. These are the people that we often refer to as "natural" or "genuine" and most everyone likes them—maybe because they're a rare breed.

It seems to me that there are very few genuine people of this sort in our world today. Most of us don't fall into this genuine camp because we are constantly on alert or on our guard. We're afraid to let our hair down, to look silly or to fail. We've developed an insatiable desire to be perfect and we work hard at trying to prove to the world that we are perfect. Since perfection is impossible, and there are no perfect people, we fool no one—at least, not for very long. You see, when we work hard at being perfect, we are really working hard at being fake—, and fake is the opposite of genuine.

Genuine people simply accept who they are and everything about them flows with life naturally. "Perfect" people swim against the flow of who they really are. In fact, they exchange their natural flow for a plastic stiffness. They glue their hair in place and brighten their teeth. They work hard at having six-pack abs and paint

their faces. They wear expensive clothing or buy expensive cars that they really can't afford. And they love to use one-upmanship as a way of bolstering their plastic self-esteem.

If we aren't feeling comfortable in our skin it's because we aren't accepting our limitations—our humanness. And we aren't believing that other people can accept our humanness—the very people who are every bit as human as we are. We're all in the same boat when it comes to our humanness. Plastic people cast judgments against others, genuine people say it like it is and accept people where they're at. Plastic people dance to the commands of others, genuine people dance to their own natural rhythms. Plastic people look outside themselves for approval, genuine people look inside themselves for approval.

- Charlie Wehrley

LOVE UNITES

*H*ow connected we are to the One Source and to each other. Do we see each other as kindred or as strangers? As friend or as foe? Are we motivated by love or fear? Love unites, fear divides. Unfortunately, fear is stronger in the hearts of most humans than love is. Instead of opening our eyes to each other, we quickly focus them on a crack in the pavement, or on the fallen leaves, or the busy squirrels, or the devouring sky-- anything to avoid human eye contact and the warmth of a smile. It's sad and disturbing. We defeat ourselves and each other through fear.

*W*hen will we, as God's children, realize that we're all siblings? We aren't threats, we're kindred. If we allowed love to rule our hearts, instead of fear, our lives would know an enduring spiritual joy; and certainly our walks down city sidewalks would be more like walks through the Kingdom on earth. Allow the light of acceptance to shake you awake from inside-out. Notice how every face around you glows with God's presence and overwhelming love: young and old, black and white, Christian and Muslim, male and female, gay and straight. We know in our souls that we are all equally loved by God, and that there are no exceptions when it comes to God's love for us all.

*F*eel it in the center of your being - this glimmer of the Divine; a glimmer of God's love, which unites us all; a glimmer that needs to become an eternal flame within each of us. And through that flame, through that eternal love for each other, we can truly be connected.

-Charlie Wehrley

LIFE ON FIRE

My life is on fire. I will not survive this life. I hunger to be fully alive for as long as I can. The growing immersion in mortality deepens my hunger to live wide awake, a staple in my spirituality. Life and the sacred awareness through which we experience it is a gift. I don't want to sleepwalk through it, or rush through it on automatic pilot.

I want to be fully conscious of every moment, every pleasure and pain, to register the magic a falling leaf imparts on October, the sadness in the cashier's eyes; to really hear my child singing herself to sleep.

– *John R. Otterbacher*

TO THINE OWN SELF BE TRUE

In facing the world, we are given two choices throughout our lives. We can be our true selves—embracing all that we consider positive and negative about ourselves— and thus attract the "right" people who are part of the support system God created for us; or we can deny our true selves— rejecting all that we consider negative about ourselves (and thus rejecting much of the positive as well) — and create a false persona to "hide" our negatives. In choosing the latter, we attract all of the "wrong" people and we attract misery into our lives. When we choose to be false, we attract no one God created to be part of our support system.

*T*hink about it. The people who were created to be significant parts of our lives won't recognize the false persona we're projecting to the world. And these are the people who are willing to accept our dark sides — all of the negatives -- as well as our light sides. In choosing to put on a false persona, which many of us do out of fear of rejection, we end up alienating all of the right people while attracting all of the wrong people. This leaves us wasting valuable time trying to change ourselves to please people we will never be able to please when we could be relaxing into our true selves with people who will love us for being our true selves.

*W*hat sense does that make? Absolutely none. So then, why are we often times making-over our natural God-given images in favor of false selves that match the images of toxic people? Why are we creating misery for ourselves instead of being our real selves for those who won't mind?

-Charlie Wehrley

FULL TO THE POINT OF BEING EMPTY

It seems there's a paradox in our culture: We are full to the point of being empty. Across America we are so full of junk culture— the garbage of our egos, of our material wants, physical desires, and personal fears— that we are empty of spiritual treasure. There's no room for it within our minds, or hearts or souls. We are preoccupied with the want of a perfect body, the lust for more money and all it can buy, and the quest for the most desirable love-life. We are satiated with food, faced with ever-expanding waistlines and faltering into poor health. And we are heavily medicated with every imaginable prescription drug. We are living self-imposed toxic lives.

We all need a time-out to get our senses back and to realize that it's time to detoxify ourselves. We need to dismiss what advertisers and peers are telling us. Once we let go of everything—social status, money, over-indulgence, fear, desires, wants, hate, material goods, all that we falsely believe we can't live without—we need to face our barrenness. We were all born barren, bereft of all ideas, dogmas, social understandings, material wants, etc. Since the day of our birth, however, we have been filling up with things. So it's time to examine ourselves; and to let go of our inner-toxins. Empty it all out. Throw out every dream, every hope, every desire, and every want that has ever made you miserable. Give them all to God.

In your stillness and barrenness, accept life on God's terms. Relax knowing you never need to struggle alone. Rest in the peacefulness of knowing your inner-turmoil is ending. Release every last impulse to control and allow God to paint a new portrait of your life. When we empty ourselves out and let go, miracles happen. Sometimes the miracles are beyond anything we could ever have imagined, and sometimes they end up being the very things that we had wanted so much.

- Charlie Wehrley

GRACE

*I*f we rely upon ourselves to carry us through our day, to be kind and attentive to our needs and the needs of others, we will find ourselves getting frustrated, impatient, judgmental, envious and angry. Self-reliance is a doorway to disaster, jealousy, and hostility. Every morning when I get up I say this little prayer to God: "Please, God, help me to do what I am capable of doing today. And help me to surrender to You that which is beyond my control. I will allow You to do for me what I cannot do for myself or others." Through this prayer I take responsibility for doing what I need to do for myself, and I allow God to do for me what I am powerless to do.

I understand that I have great difficulty being loving, charitable, merciful, and forgiving on my own. But when I accept God's graces, a door opens in my heart. It's the door to all of my vulnerable places. Once that door swings open, I find I'm able to embrace myself as God created me, just as I am, and treat myself with loving kindness. And once I'm able to do that, it's much easier to be truly loving and kind to others. It's suddenly as natural as grace itself. Meditate on your willingness to surrender yourself to God and to be thankful for God's graces today. Allow your heart to be vulnerable before God and allow your soul to shine!

- Charlie Wehrley

FEAR AND SHADOWS

"Cowards die many times before their deaths; the valiant never taste of death but once." - William Shakespeare

Fear is certainly the greatest barrier to connection with self, others and our environment. It is unclear whether modern life is more fear invoking than in simpler times past. We do know that anxiety is the most common psychological complaint and at the root of many physical illnesses. One thing we must understand about fear is that it lives **in our thoughts only** – nowhere outside our own tangles of brain tissue and wiring. Two people with differing perspectives will experience the same situation differently – one as fearful, the other as exciting or even relaxing. The difference is the power we ourselves give to our thoughts.

So, when seeking to transcend our fear we must focus outside ourselves – to move, or take action, to look outward at reality rather than inward into our thoughts. Look around you versus sinking into the mind that scans for danger. Even if it is something simple like doing the dishes or watching television – anything to pull us out of our inward focus and embrace the one moment of aliveness around us.

Fear separates us from the flow of life. We can't be alive when we are running into the past or future chased by our fears. Our life is happening in the present – in the now! We need to find our way back to our experience of here and now - This place. This time. These feelings. There is no situation that is not helped by relaxing, letting go, getting spontaneous and tuning back into our "center" in the present-tense.

-Christian R. Komor

FEAR IS USELESS

*W*e needlessly allow ourselves to be crippled by fear—far too often. And when we allow ourselves to be controlled by fear, we take the beauty out of life. For example, we're experiencing a glorious sun-filled morning as we head to the doctor's office for a check-up. We feel great, but during our evaluation we are told that we may have a serious health problem. Immediately fear strikes like lightning out of that perfectly clear-blue sky we'd been enjoying earlier. Suddenly, we don't feel great anymore, and the sky is no longer bright blue. Storm clouds are moving in wearing the face of fear. Fear snowballs into worry and worry intensifies the fear. It becomes a horrific circle that we alone perpetrate and perpetuate on ourselves. Surely, there must be some good that comes from all of this fear and worry. After all, we engage in it constantly. There must be a good purpose to it, right?

*W*ell, I can't think of a single one. Christ was right when he said fear is useless. What's needed is trust in God. What's needed is faith. Trust and fear are opposites - just as love and fear are opposites. Saint John says in his first letter that where there is love there can be no fear for love drives out fear. Faith in God also drives out fear. So we need to let go of any fear we may have. God is always with us and on our side - within each of us to bring healing to all areas of our being: mental, emotional, physical and spiritual. It takes courage and trust for us to understand this and to let go and allow God's healing energy to flow through us.

*F*ear has no power in and of itself. Fear has only the power that we give it. Think about it. Fear only exists within our minds. Embracing trust doesn't mean the problem will magically disappear overnight. Things may get worse before they get better. That's part of the natural flow of life, so we need to keep an eye on the

bigger picture. God will take care of everything if we stay away from interfering with His efforts.

*O*ne way we most interfere is by asking questions like "Why me?" There's no good answer to this question and it doesn't change anything. Instead, ask "What can I learn from this?" and look for the Light in the darkness. It's there waiting for us to discover it. Find the Light and make a positive difference for everyone around you. So let go of all fear. It's completely useless.

- Charlie Wehrley

JUST LOVE

*I*n the Gospel of John Jesus Christ asked us to "Love one another as I have loved you." - Love is the Light of the World because Love is God. God is Love. And only Love can eradicate hatred from the one world we all live in. Jesus Christ gave us two commandments: Love your God and love your neighbor as you love yourself. These two commandments are easily summed-up in one word: Love.

*W*e, ourselves, are the embodiment of love, and yet we are so drawn to clothing our hearts with hatred. We wear hatred like a cloak of protection. It's our feeble way of keeping anything we don't understand at bay. We don't understand people of a different color, or creed or sexual orientation or nationality and so we shroud ourselves in our cloaks of fear and hatred. We harbor evil thoughts toward these "different" people.

Choose instead to come from a place of discovery and acceptance. There is nothing more we need do in life to fulfill our purpose. Just love!

- Charlie Wehrley

THE DOORWAY OF GOD

*T*he divine embrace is the space where we meet our true selves through God. Naked before God we can no longer deny our imperfections, our brokenness; nor can we cruelly whip ourselves with them. Before God we see the true beauty of our being-- despite its many flaws-- and we are at peace with ourselves. Our self-hatred dissolves as we are able to see ourselves through the eyes of God, who only sees beauty in His creation. Seeing the beauty in ourselves, we too are then able to see the unique beauty in all that is God's creation. We see it in our brothers and sisters, in nature, in every aspect of life-- and best of all-- we see it through the many flaws in all that our eyes and hearts encounter. We find beauty and healing in the wounds of the world. We find healing in the heartbreak, in the sadness, and in the despair.

*M*ake your heart a holy place. Allow God to nourish your wounds by accepting your brokenness. Open yourself to the Divine Embrace. Breathe in life -- fully aware and fully alive. Then discover others in Love -- that Holy Place where all of creation unites with God -- and allow your soul to shine!

-Charlie Wehrley

GO FOR LETTING GO

We can develop the delicate balance of taking full responsibility for our lives and at the same time letting go of the unnecessary stress and busy-ness that often come from a committed and passionate life. It is this unique combination of going for it and letting go, taking responsibility and trusting that takes us beyond success to a state of artistry. There we experience a heightened awareness and a deeper connectedness to our world. May your life of work be a work of art!

– Thomas F. Crum

GRATITUDE FOR THE JOURNEY

*M*iracles can be as simple as gratitude. And yet, for many of us, gratitude can be difficult. Life's been a hard ride through numerous pitfalls for the average person. But it has also been a joyride. How is it that we so easily forget this fact? Well, it has much to do with our perspective and our ability to find mental and emotional balance. What we focus our attention on grows! And the average person seems to focus their energies on whatever daily dose of poison comes their way. There's no joy in the journey. Is it any wonder we're grumpy?

*I*nstead of griping, tomorrow let's practice gratitude for the journey. Our day will continue to be better. Get the idea? When we practice gratitude, our perspectives on life change. We realize God is trying to pull us out of our negative little mindsets and into the greater reality of His positive mindset. Focusing on positives quickly removes the cataracts from our thinking. We regain our mental and emotional balance as we weigh the positives against the negatives. We see and feel that we are blessed in numerous ways. Despite life's pitfalls, what we have in the here and now is exactly what we want or need. And all is well as we breathe sweetly and allow our souls to shine!

- Charlie Wehrley

ALL OF WHO I AM

Can I let myself experience all of who I am? Can I let go of my idolatrous relationship with thoughts, memories, and self-absorption, long enough to awaken within the world around me, within the silver finish of fish and the fur of animals and the ocean with which I am one? Can I be that still; that empty, laying down for a while the limitation of thinking about and talking about and acting out?

– John R. Otterbacher

A FORK IN THE PATH

*T*here are days when we stub our toes every few feet, and there are days when we wander off the path into flower-filled meadows or refreshing streams. Likewise, there are days when we come to a fork in the path and we aren't sure whether to go east or west. And there are times when our path seems to end and we'd much rather go backward than find our way forward into newness of life. Bad things happen to everyone. There are no exceptions. Everyone suffers. The "good" and the "bad" all suffer. When bad things happen to us we aren't being singled-out by God. No one ever promised us bad things wouldn't happen to us. When we are faced with problems along our paths, asking "why" is pointless. Even if we received an answer, it wouldn't change anything.

*I*nstead of asking "why?" we need to ask "What can I learn from this?" And we need to believe that God always wants what's best for us. Jesus never knew where he was going to lay his head at night, but he didn't play the victim. He trusted God to help him. And we can do the same. Foreclosure isn't the end of the world. We don't have to be victims. We can move forward as long as we are honest with ourselves, learn from our mistakes, and believe God is on our side. Faith in God is, simply believing God is leading us down our right path, even when we are faced with hurricanes. We will be wiser for having asked the right questions and from having learned from them. And we will be stronger for having had faith in God and for persevering despite the roughness of the storms we've faced.

-Charlie Wehrley

THE DEEP END

Please call me by my true name, so I can hear all my cries and my laughs at once, so that I can see that my joy and my pain are one. Please call me by my true name, so I can wake up, and so the doors of my heart can be left open. - Thich Nhat Hanh

There was a period in time I was doing a lot of hiking and spending most of my time just being with nature. I wasn't looking for anything in particular – just peace and connection with the Earth. In the wilderness with no one around I tended to sing much of the time. It felt like the best way of connecting with the flow of nature around me – so I sang.

And then one day I was sitting on a large lichen-speckled boulder and the most remarkable experience overtook me. (I should note that I was not taking any form of drugs or intoxicants at the time.) It was suddenly as if I was at one with all of nature around me. I became aware that I was making the clouds move and develop into their patterns; the sounds of the forest were under my direct control. Control is perhaps not the right word – more a sense of complete oneness with everything around me. Everything was in a dance – each element both act and actor. I was choosing everything that was happening around me as if I was part of it - not separate from it. I was the creator and part of the creation all at once. I was no longer a single point of personality – a unique identity with a name – I was everything and everything was me.

I wouldn't describe the experience as pleasurable, but rather as completely and totally satisfying – like being home at the end of a journey. There was nothing else to long for, strive for, or become. I just was. I was just "being." Now, coming out of the experience hours later and back into the one point of my own consciousness was quite *disturbing – a feeling of being torn from a place of utter peace and completeness back into mundane life. The experience has never happened again. I have to say it was a bit unnerving and I am not sure I would want to have it again.*

*I never spoke of the experience to anyone and, in later life. As I began my training as a psychologist I wondered if this might have been a psychotic break. If so it was the strangest one I had ever heard of. That type of mental disorder just does not happen in single, discrete, unrepeated episodes. There was no mention of such a disorder in my psychopathology texts. I **was**, however, able to find a description of similar experiences theological texts! I learned that in Zen Buddhism the experience I had was described as "Satori.".*

Satori means "to see one's essence or nature." D. T. Suzuki is credited with bringing the study of Zen to America. Suzuki says Satori has these characteristics: "Those who have experienced it are always at a loss to explain it coherently or logically; Satori involves an intuitive insight into the essence of one's nature; the individual is aware of the finality of the experience and no amount of logical argument can refute it. Being direct and personal the experience is sufficient unto itself. All that logic can do is to explain it, to interpret it in connection to other kinds of knowledge with which our minds are filled; It is an affirmative experience accepting and appreciating all things that exist as they come along regardless of their moral values; There is a powerful sense of the Beyond - the experience of being one's self but with a feeling it is rooted elsewhere." (D.T. Suzuki, 1982)

The shell in which the individual personality is so solidly encased explodes at the moment of Satori - individuality, rigidly held together and definitely kept separate from other individual existences, becomes loosened somehow and melts away into an indescribable oneness on a different order from what one is accustomed to. The feeling that follows is that of complete release or a complete rest---the feeling that one has arrived finally at the destination.

The experience of satori is reported in all cultures regardless of religious beliefs or practices; Satori brings a feeling of exaltation. That this feeling inevitably accompanies Satori is due to the fact that it is the breaking-up of the restriction imposed on one as an individual being - an infinite expansion of the individual; And finally that Satori comes upon one abruptly and is a brief experience. In fact, if it is not abrupt and momentary, it is not Satori.

I share this story as there seems to be agreement dating back to the origins of humankind that our true state of being is in deep connection with everything else around us. From my point of view, as a western author, it was as if I had been briefly returned to the Biblical Garden of Eden where, it is said, humans existed in direct connection with nature, - rather than the separate and individual points of consciousness we normally experience.

Looking back on this powerful experience I can see how, without this sense of deep connectedness to our Earth and our fellow beings we all become mere commodities in the struggle for survival. From a place of infinite connection we are drawn naturally to support, love and nurture every being, every animal, every plant, and every rock as part of us.

- Christian R. Komor

PEACE

If I am not at peace with myself, how can I be at peace with my neighbor? I can't be. It's impossible. Peace has to truly begin with me. This means that I must work on loving, accepting, and forgiving myself. Once I can empathize with me, I can empathize with others. Once I befriend my own brokenness, I can befriend the brokenness of family members, friends, neighbors, co-workers, etc. Peace begins within me and it spreads across my world; uniting with the peace that others have attained in their own hearts.

Imagine people learning to listen better to each other. Picture people learning to agree to disagree about things they can't see eye to eye on, and in doing so, envision them as they come to see and respect the image and likeness of God that each of them projects to the world.

Everyone gets hurt. We all face betrayal, gossip, lies, infidelities, and the pain of being victimized by people -- even those we once loved and trusted. Asking "why me?" is never a solution. It's pointless and so is harboring a grudge. A grudge or resentment is a vial of emotional poison. When we allow personal wounds to fester into resentments, we betray ourselves by swallowing the emotional poison we've concocted to kill our perpetrator.

Grievances exist only in our thoughts and emotions. I am choosing to forever give you power over me and my life by refusing to forgive you." The only way we can take our power back from the offending person is by forgiving them. Forgiveness requires that we revisit the wound with the intent of allowing ourselves to honestly feel the hurt we've repressed. Tears help to release the sadness and bring us back to wholeness. Then we are able to forgive and take back our power.

The choice is ours: healing or perpetual suffering. Holding on to resentment gives us a false sense of power that always explodes, wounding no one but us. Forgiveness sets the perpetrator of our grievance free, and more importantly, it sets us free: Free of anger, rage, hatred and victimization.

- Charlie Wehrley

LET GO

*L*et go of who you think you are, the form, thoughts, identity, intensity, longing, roles, flesh, and bone. Let go of everything that seems to be you, and experience who you most deeply are. Not just the form, but the energy that lends itself to form. The Spirit that pounds within your heart, but throbs as well in the ocean swells, in the fish and seabirds, which pulses in the sun and wind. Can you die enough to who you think you are to experience who you also are? Can you?

— John R. Otterbacher

PETS ON FACEBOOK

"There is not a sprig of grass that shoots uninteresting to me." – Thomas Jefferson

There is an interesting phenomena happening. As a culture and a planet we have more communication choices than ever before and yet how many people do you know who can really say they have and give all the friendship and love they need and want? How many people do you know who can say they are at peace with their intimate relationships – if they even have them? We are creatures with so much "love potential" and yet we seem to be living in a "love void". Look at all those Facebook Friends! We are connected and yet...so often not.

Relationships are at the apex of the human experience – complex, fascinating, difficult and challenging. With such big risks and big rewards some fumbling and wandering down blind alleys is unavoidable. But we humans also have a tendency to avoid what is difficult. Avoidance means finding a distraction a "medicator" or substitute for what we fear – and alcohol and drugs are only the most obvious examples. The challenges of relating can lead us to turn to a pet who will, of course, give us unconditional love. The same is true of social networking on the computer – we can alter, fabricate, create, wave a magic mouse and presto! – we have hundreds of "friends". Pets and pixels can give us the illusion of relatedness.

True love and connection are **out there** on the street – in the connection that happens between real flesh and blood human beings. How many times do we end the day with the feeling that we gave and received all the love available? How often can we say our cup was filled and we filled all the cups of the others we encountered - that everyone you came in contact with got all they needed? Do you feel an abundance of love circulating? I bet not.

The real world needs your love - in fact it is aching for your love! Animals are wonderful - to be protected and preserved – but they are not human. With few exceptions *they can survive without our love and sometimes are even harmed by it. Operating on instinct and genetic programming animals live blissfully ignorant of the challenges of self-awareness and of conscious relationship. Computers have amazing capabilities and can perform wondrous feats, but they are inorganic bits and bytes – not at all part of the web of life. We can share information through their portals, but not real hand-to-hand connection.*

Are we creating a void of love where there could be abundance – more than enough love-loaves and friendship-fishes for everyone to eat their fill!? I think the answer is yes, and it is placing our increasingly interdependent society at great, and yet unseen, risk. As the social world spins faster - without a web of true flesh and blood connection to hold things together we are in danger of spinning out of control.

This just won't do! Go out into the street right now today and find someone to give your love to. You have a precious gift within you and gifts are meant to be given. Yes, be sure to hug your pet before you grab your keys and check your e-mail, but don't let them take the place of real love and real connection.

- Christian Komor

SURROUNDED BY THE WARMTH OF GOD'S LOVE

When the Lord established the heavens I was there...and I was his delight day by day, playing before him all the while, playing on the surface of his earth; and I found delight in the human race. (Book of Proverbs)

God delights in us. So why don't we believe it? Maybe it's because we fail to delight in ourselves. When we look in a mirror, we don't readily see ourselves as the delightful stars of God's favorite show. Instead, we take a brief look and say "I'm just not pretty enough" or "I'm just not talented enough," or "I'm just not clever enough" for God to delight in me.

We all need to see ourselves through the eyes of a child, as God does. Children don't see black or white, fat or skinny, ugly or beautiful. They don't see wrinkles, gray hair, or big hips. Likewise, they don't judge anyone as smart or stupid. When children look at us, all they see is beauty. All they see is someone they love. They see only goodness much the same way as God does. God looks at all creation and proclaims it good.

Let's honestly try to see ourselves through the God-like eyes of a child. We will be enraptured by what we see: the coolest, cleverest, most delightful person on earth. We'll glow from within, surrounded by the warmth of God's love.

- Charlie Wehrley

THREE DEEP BREATHS

We become so consumed by perceived competition and the obsession with doing that we multitask our way right out of the present moment. How do we find our way back home in today's world? The way is profound and yet simple. Right in the moment we can take a few conscious breaths. The first breath can calm and soothe your body, the second can restore the tranquility of your mind, and the third can reunite you with the spirit.

– Thomas F. Crum

THE ESSENTIAL BLISS OF BEING LOVED FOR WHO WE ARE

We all have basic inherent human needs and it's essential that we honor them. Human growth requires more than bread and water, more than exercise and sleep, more than warm clothing and a comfortable chair. It requires more than sexual ecstasy and intellectual enlightenment. It even requires more than a spiritual connection to a Higher Power. The most basic human need, the one that must be fulfilled for healthy human growth, is the need to be loved and accepted for who we are.

*T*here are too many of us in this world who have never known the essential bliss of being loved and accepted for who we are. We've known the desire since we were old enough to reach out and hug our parents. We've longed to hear the words "I love you just as you are," and we've longed to feel the warmth of such unconditional acceptance through the embrace of another. But it's rarely - if ever - happened.

*I*n taking this path, we placed ourselves at the mercy of the outside world. We allowed others to decide if we were OK or not. This caused us tremendous emotional pain, and it sometimes forced us to sell our souls for the sake of someone else's approval. We sometimes became chameleons. Worst yet, the approval we most often received was for being who the other person wanted us to be, not for being who we really are. So we continued to run on emotional empty - year after year after year; continually looking to the wrong people to fill us up. Only we can fill our emotional tank. It's time to look inside ourselves again. Love and acceptance begin with "me."

*I*f we want to be loved and accepted for who we are, we have to be the first to say "YES!" to ourselves. We have to be the first to hug ourselves into the warmth of feeling loved and accepted just the way we are. Once we decide it's good to be genuinely who we are, we will begin to experience true love and acceptance from others. They will mirror it to us through their eyes and

we will feel it in the warmth of their touch. They will mirror it to us through their eyes and we will feel it in the warmth of their touch. And we may even hear it in words that emanate from their hearts. Begin today by offering yourself unconditional love and acceptance. Fulfill your own most basic human need to the fullest. Feel yourself glow from within and feel the warmth of God's smile upon you. Invite others to share this new-found love with you, and allow your soul to shine!

- Charlie Wehrley

RETURN TO THE GARDEN

"Love is all you need." – John Lennon

What kind of conversations do you have with yourself? If you're like many of us your conversations are harsh, blaming, and laced with self-criticism. "Well, that was dumb." "I know they won't like me." "What's going to go wrong next?" We learn this sort of conversation in a competitive, un-accepting, fear-based world where love is viewed as a short-supply commodity. A byproduct of this lack of self-acceptance is a dampening down of our aliveness, spontaneity and joy in the experience of living. Without self-love we are too inhibited, too serious, clinging too tightly to the approval of others.

In the story of the Garden of Eden humans were separated from animals by our self-consciousness. We ate from the tree of knowledge and became self-aware and self-judging. We became capable of shame and self-condemnation. The rest of nature went on without us – behavior perfectly aligned with itself – perfectly accepting – completely absent of judgment. We are the only creatures on Earth who need to <u>learn</u> how to love ourselves. We must re-teach ourselves how to speak to our own self with acceptance and unconditional self-love. This does not mean the entitlement which today so often masquerades as self-esteem.

As we re-learn that - far from the rare commodity we imagined - love is an endless spring and we are naturally drawn to share that spring with our thirsty fellows. True self-love leads us to share. We naturally "love our neighbor <u>as</u> ourselves" and we bring our inner healing out into the world.

*S*o start with listening to how you talk with yourself and then notice what patterns of negative self-talk there are. Shift them to the positive, the kind, the loving. If you can't quite get the hang of it at first, love yourself for that! Imagine that you are completely wrapped in the arms of acceptance. Remember that love chases out fear. Practice feeling self-love and your awareness of being confident and sure in the world will grow. Pride and contentment will grow as you love what and who you are rather than trying to become what you are not. Like the one who created your essence, you will love **everything** about you, **everything** you do, and **everything** that you are.

- Christian R. Komor

THIS SWEET MOMENT

"And this, our life, exempt from public haunt, finds tongues in trees, books in the running brooks, sermons in stones, and good in everything" - William Shakespeare

There is a great challenge and a fear buried deep at the bottom of all the other layers of involved in Being human. The challenge - to really live in the awareness of how precious and wonderful life is. The fear - being truly alive – and more than that, letting others <u>see</u> you are alive!

We are talking about being TRULY alive, not the shuffling zombie-like existence many of us experience. Truly ALIVE! So alive that our exuberance - our pure desire for life - is unmistakable to others. Surmounting this fear requires us to expand our awareness into the future where we find the awareness of the finality of life. There is a finite amount of time from cradle to grave. In between are all these incredibly special people and experiences. Such awareness is overwhelmingly sweet and powerful.

It is easy to be overwhelmed with the sacredness and intensity of Being truly alive. It is so easy to give in to the fear of really celebrating – fear of really saying "my life is now!" How strange to be afraid of what most of us would say we long for the most. Odd that it is so hard to open up to aliveness – yet one meets very, very few people who can make this leap. How many of the problems in our world are due to the shrinking away from the experience of enjoyment of life? How different our world might be if not for the fear of aliveness.

-Christian R. Komor

LIFE TURNS OUT AS IT DOES

"And the day came when the risk it took to remain tight inside the bud was more painful than the risk it took to blossom." – Anais Nin

Have you ever noticed that life turns out as it does – not as we expect it will or want it to. Sure, sometimes the realities of life and our expectations and plans match up, but more often you just never know what you're going to find around the next corner.

As we learn this we develop a grace in living - a stillness in the midst of motion in which we can be non-judgmental. How can we "judge" events when we don't know which will lead to pleasure and which to suffering in the course of time? We may be able to see the crack in the sidewalk right in front of us, but certainly not what is over the next rise. We can but look at it all with peacefully detached interest – taking things lightly and remembering that what will be, will be. Life turns out as it does.

– Christian R. Komor

DOGGEDLY CHOOSE LOVE

Thomas Merton once began a prayer, 'Dear God, I have no idea where I am going.' He could have added, 'I don't have to.' I can follow the path of love even when I don't know where it leads. Whatever my circumstances or emotional state – sad, mad, scared or serene – I can doggedly choose to love. I can obstinately hold to love as long as I have life, confidant that love alchemizes everything, transforms everything.

– John R. Otterbacher

ACCEPT EVERYTHING

"If you are not concerned about the outcome of a circumstance, you will experience no fear. Whatever the outcome will be, will be, whether you fear it or not." -
Ching Ning Chu

*A*lways strive to come from discovery and acceptance rather than judgment and criticism. What seems to be a gift today may become a burden tomorrow. What seems to be a joy today may be a sorrow in days to come. Our ship is already chartered to travel between our home port of birth and that undiscovered country of death. As we travel the course we are free to make choices how to spend our days on deck, but in the larger context of the journey we cannot tell blessing from curse. To judge and criticize, then, is egotistical folly. Dance with this moment, this day, this place.

*I*n our world there are so many different perspectives, values and ways of being that no one position can be the "right" one, so the KEY THING is, are you someone who is curious, interested, accepting, tolerant and non-judgmental towards others ways of thinking and being, or are you intolerant, closed-minded and judgmental? That is the real question and the deciding point in a relationship. If you can't get the acceptance thing, no relationship is ever going to work because no one is going to think and behave just like you.

*W*hen you think about it we often feel we are somehow "special" – different from everyone else - as if we are not facing the same random risks in life that everyone else is. We yearn for something to make us feel *perfectly* safe *always*. Escaping risk leads to greater (real) risk. There is often less danger in the things we fear than in the things we desire. Free yourself by realizing you are just a

normal human being. Celebrate that! Good things and bad things will happen in your life and, yes, this physical life does end. Celebrate being part of a community of human beings suffering – AND rejoicing! No one leaves here alive.

For what we resist grows stronger and, of course, one thing that many of us resist is illness, disease, and death. It's difficult and challenging to be sure, but we need to slowly make friends with the truth and we will, one day, no longer be on this planet in this body. Often when we get into trouble in our minds it is because we are rebelling against the **idea** of death – not necessarily death itself – after all, we can only really die once and obviously today was not that day! Make friends with it – it happens to everyone after all. And whatever happens afterward can't be all that "bad". The choices seem to be; nothing, reincarnation, Heaven, or merging with universal energy. Unless you believe in a Hell you're going to be okay not matter what!

If you're accepting, then there is nothing to fear! And better still - whatever death may be for us when it comes – <u>today</u> it is a blessed teacher reminding us not to take anything here too seriously, while at the same time knowing it's okay to take risks, to have adventures and new experiences. So many of us live as if we are expecting our lives to go on forever. The world is here to be experienced with an open mind and heart. Our personal gifts and talents are here to be given in service of that which will add love, kindness and health to our world. Live, give and enjoy THIS day!

-Christian R. Komor

LET GOD GO FIRST

"If you listen to your fears, you will die never knowing what a great person you might have been." - Robert H. Schuller

There is a wonderful old adage which emerged from desert cultures, "Trust God...and tie your camel!" - and from further to the north "God grant me the serenity to accept the things I cannot change, the courage to change the things I can and the wisdom to know the difference." The thinking is sound. Know the difference between what you can do something about, and what is best to let go of. Ask God (The Universe, Destiny) to lead and **you** follow. So often we ask for help and then continue trying to do it ourselves anyway. We forget the second part of asking for assistance which is **accepting** that assistance – especially when it is Divine assistance we seek!

If we keep one foot in tomorrow and one foot in yesterday we step over today. Things turn out best for people who play the cards they receive each day. God deals the cards – not us. Our fear wants us to live in the past and tremble for the future, but both are in hands more sure and powerful than ours. Peace can only be found in **this moment** here and now.

When we get off course in life God will let us know. You will never feel okay if you are not okay! If you feel angry, lost, not yourself – these feelings are how we are guided back toward our own true self. It is as if the Universe will keep pestering us until we "get it right" in terms of being congruent with ourselves. Rejoice in the discomfort of being off course – it is a gift that guides us back home.

– *Christian R. Komor*

FORGIVENESS

What is breath without air? What is life without love? And what is love without forgiveness? One has no purpose without the other. Yet, we often fail at being resurrected spiritually because we fail to take breaths that are true, we fail to live on life's oasis of love and we fail to love ourselves well enough to forgive and to accept forgiveness.

Loving well begins with loving one's self well (unconditionally). And loving one's self well leads to forgiving one's self. Yet, almost everywhere I spoke, people told me of their inability to forgive themselves. It was obvious to me that the past still haunts many people because they don't love themselves well enough to forgive themselves for the mistakes of their yesterdays.

There's no good reason for failing to forgive yourself. God has already forgiven you for the past. All you have to do to receive this forgiveness is to ask for it. God's forgiveness is never denied you no matter what you've done. There's really only one reason why people can't forgive themselves and that reason is this They choose not to forgive themselves. And they choose not to forgive themselves because their self-love is so poor that they don't see themselves as worthy of love or forgiveness.

We hear a lot about carrying your crosses in life. But there's a big difference between carrying a cross and nailing yourself to it. Shit happens. And it happens to everyone without exception. Sometimes that shit, which we have no power over, is a cross we need to bear. And we can bear it well by understanding the wisdom and the fruits that bearing these crosses provide us with as we journey through life. We don't have to nail ourselves to these crosses, though, by playing the victim or the martyr. People who play *these roles never see the wisdom gained by their suffering and so it never produces fruit or grace.*

Whenever we refuse to see ourselves as an image and likeness of the Divine, we choose to love ourselves poorly. And we choose to open the door to self-deprecation. We then choose to criticize ourselves—and every mistake we make—without mercy. We beat ourselves up and come to believe we are unworthy of love and forgiveness and all that's good in life.

The more you choose to love yourself well, the easier you will find it to be gentle with yourself when you make mistakes. And the easier you will find it in your heart to truly forgive yourself for the past. If you are having trouble with removing the self-imposed nails of your own self-hatred, ask a Higher Power to help you. Remember, you were created by God and so you already possess God's stamp of approval. Now, all you need is your own. God loves you just the way you are and so you have no excuse for refusing to love yourself in the same way. It's your choice. You can choose to love, accept and forgive your humanness, or you can choose to hate, reject and condemn it. Why would anyone choose the latter, when the first option is so readily available?

Ask God for the grace to heal the wounds you have imposed on yourself, choose to love who you are and then choose to set yourself free of the past through the great grace of forgiveness. Forgive yourself, graciously accept the forgiveness of God and others, and truly allow the glow of Resurrection to light your spiritual path before you.

- Charlie Wehrley

INSTINCT AND KNOWING

Birds sing after a storm; why shouldn't people feel as free to delight in whatever remains to them? - Rose Kennedy

The voice of God speaks throughout all of nature.

Having been left behind when we humans were ejected from the "Garden of Eden," animals hear this voice of instinct and inner knowing easily. They shift their behavior patterns without a thought from season to season. Fish return upstream to spawn. Birds and sea creatures migrate over great distances in specific patterns. Even insects perform their dance in choreographed and highly interconnected patterns.

Far from the simplicity of Eden - having chosen knowledge and control over connection with nature - we humans rely on our brains and machines. We have radar and satellites to navigate our travels and tell us the weather outside, clocks and calendars to inform our preparations for winter or spring, and media to tell us what clothing to wear. Gradually we have lost touch with the voice of God which still speaks softly to us through instinct and intuition. We have taught ourselves not to listen to our "gut".

Though it is hard to imagine a complete return to the Garden, we can, however, reawaken our senses. Even now amongst all of the noise and activity of our highly compressed, machine-dominated age. We can choose to remain still long enough to begin to catch enlightening glimmers of Heavenly-wisdom trickling through our cluttered brain-static… instinctual inner-knowing, our most direct connection with God.

– *Christian R. Komor*

216 | EARTHSPIRIT!

THE MONK AND THE WILD HORSES

In ancient days, near China's northern borders, lived an old Monk who owned a fabulous stallion. Though the stallion would fetch a great price, the man would never sell his beloved horse. All the people of his village were envious of this most beautiful possession. The old man, on the other hand, would simply smile and say to any admirers, "Yes, this horse is most beautiful, but whether it is good fortune or bad that it is with me I could not say." Everyone in the village thought he was just being modest which made them all the more envious and jealous.

One day his horse wandered into the territory of the northern tribes. Everyone commiserated with him, "You were too greedy. You should have sold your horse and pocketed the money. Now your horse is lost forever and you have nothing." The Monk replied, "I have not thought of good or bad fortune. My horse has been lost. That is all I know for certain. A curse or a blessing, who can say?"

Some weeks later a cry went up in the village. The monk's horse had returned - bringing with him a small herd of wild horses from the north. All the people of the village now came to congratulate the Monk on his great luck. "Good fortune you say" observed the Monk, "Perhaps yes, perhaps no. All I can say for sure is that my horse has returned and brought with him many other horses."

Since he was now well-off as the owner of many good horses the Monk adopted a son. The Monk and the boy became very close and shared many happy days together. Then one day his son fell from a horse he was training and broke

his thigh bone quite severely. Everyone commiserated with the old Monk. "Your son will be crippled for life; you will have no one to continue managing your horses and take care of you in your old age." The Monk just looked at them, shook his head and replied, "Misfortune or blessing I cannot say. All I know for certain is that my son has fallen and is now crippled."

A short time later the northern tribes began a massive invasion of the border regions. All able-bodied young men were pressed into military service and took up arms to fight against the invaders. As the northern tribes were far advanced in numbers and weaponry, it was almost certain that none of the young men from the village would return alive. But the Monk's son, being crippled, was unable to go to the fight and remained home. Now, the villagers came to the Monk with envy saying, "What luck you have! Your son cannot join in the fighting because he is crippled and so will survive."

Once more the Monk looked at his friends with compassion and shook his head, "Why can you not give up your attachment to the judgment of events? Misfortune or blessing, I cannot say. I only know that my son is crippled and here with me now." With this the villager's eyes were finally opened and many of them began to study with the Monk and seek his counsel.

If we cannot know the eventual outcome of things then how can we really judge very much or criticize? As sometimes-rational Beings our best course is to consider all events as adventures, and foster a blissful acceptance of all people, places, and events... including ourselves!

- Adapted by Christian R. Komor

AFTERWARD: BIG TROUBLE ON LITTLE EARTH

"A good head and a good heart are always a formidable combination." - Nelson Mandela

It is our cherished hope as authors that you will feel empowered by these writings to take whatever steps are available to you to love and care for your, neighbors, our planet and yourself! We all exist in **connection** to our precious Earth and to one another, and without that connection we are all truly lost. Humankind is capable of an expansive range of behavior, from nearly divine self-sacrifice to genocide. As the population of our Earth and the interconnectedness of our problems increase, everyone senses big trouble is brewing. We may not prevail against these challenges, but let's at least put up a heck of a fight!

Whether placed here on this planet by a deity, evolution or both, the entirety of our human civilization, in the 4.6 billion year journey of our planet, is a page or two in the flip-book of existence. To date our planet has already experienced no less than two cataclysmic environmental disasters wiping out most of life on Earth! The first around 245 million years ago (cause unknown), and a second 65 million years ago (caused by the impact of a comet or meteor only six miles in diameter which struck the Yucatan Peninsula). Each of these global disasters extinguished between 70 and 90 percent of Earth's species! The Earth survived, but it's inhabitants largely did not.

Today, in the crowded doorway, to the 22nd Century, humans seem to be preparing to create our own cataclysm in the form of a powerful, interconnected escalation of human-borne disasters. At any one time on the globe there are around 100 wars in progress with a cumulative total of 1,605,500 deaths per year. This does not include the "major conflicts" such as World War II which alone led to a worldwide total of 22.6

million military dead and also contributed significantly to the 20th century death-by-genocide total of 36 million persons exterminated.

In 2010 there were close to 10,000 homicides committed in the United States (ranking us just behind South Africa, Columbia, and Thailand). In the same year, 14 out of every 100,000 persons on the planet murdered themselves (this figure does not include medical DNR requests), an increase beyond the understanding or expectations of the scientific community. In addition, as a result of the toxification of our environment, allergies, certain types of cancers, and a number of neurobiological disorders have increased exponentially. Meanwhile, with the advent of air travel, communicable disease has expanded its' reach. During the 20th century, somewhere between, 145-350 million persons have died of AIDS, tuberculosis and malaria alone.

And then there is Global Climate Change. Politics aside, the Earth's climate is in a long term warming phase that began when the last ice age ended about 20-25 thousand years ago. (The next ice age is expected to begin in about twice that time.)

The main triggers for cooling and warming trends have always been the small, regular variations in the geometry of the Earth's orbit around the sun which affects the distribution of solar radiation at the Earth's surface. In addition, however, over the past 200 years, human activities have increased the amount of carbon dioxide in the atmosphere by over 30%. This is well beyond the range of its natural variation during the last million years or more. If the increase continues and if adequate action is not taken to stem it, the atmospheric carbon dioxide content will soon reach double its' pre-industrial value. This will, in turn, raise world temperatures via the "greenhouse effect".

*E*ven if this rise in temperature is only 2.5°C, it will represent about half an 'ice-age' in terms of climate change. For this to occur in less than 100 years is catastrophic and will primarily be experienced as extreme weather disruption.

*T*his climate/weather disruption will place extreme stress on an already overpopulated planet. In 2010 the United Nations reported that over 42 million people had been displaced as a result of sudden onset disasters - of which 90 percent have been displaced by climate-related disasters. (This does not include the growing number of persons affected by drought.) In a single incident, the Russian Heat Wave of 2010, over 56,000 people perished.

*M*any of our difficulties, including global pollution, trace back to the rapid expansion of our world population. In many ways we are simply asking our global

ecosystem to do too much for us. The world's population has doubled (100% increase) in 40 years from 1959 (3 billion) to 1999 (6 billion). It is now estimated that in another 40 years or so it will increase by another 50%, to become 9 billion – the equivalent of the addition of two Chinas!

In all animal models, overpopulation such as this correlates with an increase in antisocial and anarchistic behavior. This is certainly true for humans. In 2009 alone, approximately 11,000 terrorist attacks occurred in 83 countries resulting in over 58,000 victims, including nearly 15,000 fatalities. Since the dawn of our current century, large portions of the population have lost faith in the positive progress of evolution. Pervasive doubt has emerged in the ability of our governments, religions, financial institutions, and corporate-industrial monopolies to create a peaceful thriving global culture. It is no longer unusual to find someone willing to "tear it all down and start over" using the most terrifying and violent means they have at their disposal.

*A*nd so, there is indeed big trouble on our little planet and it seems to be growing in proportion to our imaginations, which are both wondrous and relatively uncontrolled. Until recently we have been busily creating the instruments of our own destruction without much thought to more than our immediate comforts and profitability. (Interestingly, with all we have sacrificed to attain superior healthcare and a high standard of living the United States ranks 36th among nations in terms of longevity – behind Cuba, South Korea, Singapore, Macau, and most of the leading countries of the world.) Again, we have to ask – what is wrong with this picture and why aren't we fixing it?

It may shock you when I suggest that one of the chief architects of our rush to self-destruction was a man named Henry Ford. To be fair Henry certainly must not have envisioned the scope of death and destruction which would be wrought by mass production of the automobile and its combustion engine. Automobiles directly kill approximately 1.3 million people globally each year and 20-50 million more are seriously injured.

This is especially true for our children. Traffic injuries are by far the leading cause of death for teens. This means, in America, 9 teens die and 960 are hospitalized every day (150 every hour) as a result of traffic accidents.

And then there's those pesky carbon emissions. There are two main types of pollution discharged by fossil fuel powered vehicles, exhaust emission including dangerous gases such as carbon monoxide, oxides of nitrogen, hydrocarbons and particulates and evaporative emissions - vapors of fuel which are released into the atmosphere, without being burnt. Both cause massive and widespread pollution of our environment on a scale which eclipses all other sources combined! Fossil fuel combustion, particularly as it occurs in motor vehicles, has been identified as the **largest single contributor** *to air pollution in the world and directly linked via biomarker data to genetic damage, cancer mortality, and cardiopulmonary and cardiovascular disease. Factories that are associated with automobile manufacturing have also had a significant negative environmental impact.*

*We continue to feed our healthcare system billions upon billions of dollars in a search for causes and cures to the diseases which plague humankind. Yet somehow we continue to remain unaware that we will be **driving that very cause** merrily down the road later today! Our collective denial is, of course, helped along by those who profit from our blindness. One can almost imagine a collection of CEO's praying fervently, that no one looks up from their steering wheel long enough to see the bigger picture. Amazingly, few of us equate the combustion engine as a primary cause of major health problems and the rapid degradation of our natural environment and yet it is hard to argue otherwise.*

We already know the way to fix much of what is threatening our precious Earth! We must check population growth and do so immediately. We no longer have the luxury for arcane beliefs. Only so many people can fit in the boat before it sinks and once it sinks, there will be no more life. We have already learned much about how to utilize and retain energy in more "green" and efficient ways. We must mandate energy efficiency across the board including clear and understandable product labeling which shows an efficiency rating - money saved and pollution avoided. We must redirect subsidies from "big oil" to "big solar", "big wind", and other renewable sources. We must rethink our neighborhoods and cities to facilitate walking, cycling, and public transportation and make this attractive to those with choices. We must ramp up recycling, which has huge climate benefits compared with burning trash.

When it comes to transportation there are plenty of simple, inexpensive, even cost-free and enjoyable ways for modern motorists to cut their carbon output – driving less (by walking, cycling or using public transport as much as possible), combining trips, car-pooling, and by changing one's driving style (for instance, not racing to red lights but approaching them slowly so the lights might change to green, to minimize idling). One can buy a more efficient car, maybe even a used one, as so much energy is consumed building cars. And of course one might even choose, on occasion to drive more – instead of flying in carbon-spewing jets.

Most critically we must promote cultural norms such as those in EarthSpirit! that value health, education, and social well-being over mindless consumption.

To make these fundamental changes we need to engage people – not as consumers but as citizens. That's where our real power to make change exists. We must vote with our wallets. We must let our elected officials know we want clean, safe energy. We want efficiency. We want innovation. We want action – to turn away from the dirty energy choices of the past and turn toward the clean energy economy where our only viable future lies.

We have seen the power of an idea whose time has come. For the idea of Earth Preservation to be more than another fad or corporate gimmick, we need **connection**. *We need to have our feet, or at least our minds,* **out on the land**. *Our sincere hope is that EarthSpirit! and her sister books "Driving Ourselves Sane" and "The Power of Being" will be such a connection for you and for those you share it with - bringing the land, sky and waters home to your heart…and rekindling your EarthSpirit!*

www.ingramcontent.com/pod-product-compliance
Lightning Source LLC
Chambersburg PA
CBHW040902020526
44114CB00037B/32